Y0-ARB-554

NEW DIRECTIONS FOR STUDENT SERVICES

Margaret J. Barr, *Northwestern University*
EDITOR-IN-CHIEF

M. Lee Upcraft, *The Pennsylvania State University*
ASSOCIATE EDITOR

Total Quality Management: Applying Its Principles to Student Affairs

William A. Bryan
University of North Carolina at Wilmington

EDITOR

Number 76, Winter 1996

JOSSEY-BASS PUBLISHERS
San Francisco

TOTAL QUALITY MANAGEMENT: APPLYING ITS PRINCIPLES
TO STUDENT AFFAIRS
William A. Bryan (ed.)
New Directions for Student Services, no. 76
Margaret J. Barr, Editor-in-Chief
M. Lee Upcraft, Associate Editor

Microfilm copies of issues and articles are available in 16mm and 35mm,
as well as microfiche in 105mm, through University Microfilms Inc., 300
North Zeeb Road, Ann Arbor, Michigan 48106-1346.

ISSN 0164-7970   ISBN 0-7879-9932-6

NEW DIRECTIONS FOR STUDENT SERVICES is part of The Jossey-Bass Higher
and Adult Education Series and is published quarterly by Jossey-Bass Inc.,
Publishers, 350 Sansome Street, San Francisco, California 94104-1342.
Periodicals postage paid at San Francisco, California, and at additional
mailing offices. POSTMASTER: Send address changes to New Directions for
Student Services, Jossey-Bass Inc., Publishers, 350 Sansome Street, San
Francisco, California 94104-1342.

SUBSCRIPTIONS cost $52.00 for individuals and $79.00 for institutions,
agencies, and libraries.

EDITORIAL CORRESPONDENCE should be sent to the Editor-in-Chief,
Margaret J. Barr, 633 Clark Street, 2-219, Evanston, Illinois 60208-1103.

Cover photograph by Wernher Krutein/PHOTOVAULT © 1990.

TCF Manufactured in the United States of America on Lyons Falls
Pathfinder Tradebook. This paper is acid-free and 100 percent
totally chlorine-free.

CONTENTS

EDITOR'S NOTES

Higher education institutions are increasing their commitment to continuous improvement and many are applying total quality management (TQM) principles to their campuses. Some educators view TQM as a fad that will soon disappear. Dissatisfaction with educational outcomes is increasing, however, and demands for higher levels of quality from academic institutions are being made. With the cost of a degree spiraling out of the reach of many prospective students, public scrutiny of how higher education functions intensifies. As always, higher education professionals must listen and respond to criticism and dissatisfaction. Educators must invite review, study their processes, and involve many constituencies in their continuous quality improvement efforts.

Since the late 1980s many academic institutions have sought to implement TQM, either as a comprehensive campus agenda or within selected campus administrative units. A review of the literature reveals many good examples of TQM and a plethora of definitions of TQM. For some, it is a management panacea that allows a campus to do more with fewer resources while continuing to provide quality services; although this may be an outcome of TQM in some settings, this is not the primary reason for implementing TQM. TQM is a comprehensive approach that strives for continuous quality improvement in all work processes. Higher education is currently in an era of intense public examination. Educational leaders must be good stewards of public funding and must constantly look for more efficient ways of doing their work.

TQM principles are not new to student affairs divisions; nor is the term "customer." Student affairs professionals must become more knowledgeable about the comprehensive nature of TQM, however, and must know how to apply principles to functional work areas in divisions of student affairs. This volume, *Total Quality Management: Applying Its Principles to Student Affairs,* attempts to provide an overview of TQM-related information for student affairs professionals and tries to sensitize them to issues surrounding its use. It also provides examples of TQM application in a student affairs setting. This sourcebook is intended for student affairs professionals—especially chief student affairs officers and program directors—and can be useful for other university officials, including presidents.

The authors in this volume present differing perspectives regarding what TQM is or is not and how it can be applied or adapted to the work of student affairs professionals. The volume's general focus is an examination of TQM (advantages and disadvantages) and what it might offer student affairs professionals as they continuously strive for quality student learning opportunities, student development initiatives, and student services—wholesale acceptance or rejection of TQM is avoided.

In Chapter One, I explore TQM and the various themes, tools, and beliefs that make it different from other management approaches. Deming's fourteen points (principles) are presented with a restatement of each principle for the student affairs setting. Observations and reasons for TQM's popularity are outlined.

Chapter Two examines the realities—negative and positive—of attempting to implement TQM in student affairs departments. Nancy Lee Howard discusses three positive applications of TQM at Oregon State University in the admissions office, student union, and financial aid office. She outlines important steps toward maximizing the success of TQM in student affairs.

Tyrone A. Holmes examines the weaknesses of current TQM efforts in Chapter Three, including a discussion of the problems inherent with TQM initiatives in an educational environment. Strategies for the effective application of TQM concepts are discussed, with a particular focus on ACPA's Student Learning Imperative and its confluence with TQM philosophy.

In Chapter Four, Richard H. Mullendore and Li-Shing Wang outline a comprehensive planning model for student affairs divisions that integrates TQM principles with resource allocation, assessment efforts, and annual reports. The process involved in creating this model is also discussed.

In Chapter Five, D. David Ostroth describes a systematic approach used in one student affairs department to introduce TQM training, strategies, and style into the organization's culture. He discusses how a systematic approach provided a framework for the successful integration of continuous improvement philosophy and techniques into the perennial style of one student affairs department.

Assessment can be used to determine how quality is achieved in student affairs programs and services. In Chapter Six, Richard M. Scott gives examples of the importance of assessment in TQM. He stresses the importance of articulating how institutions and student affairs divisions are producing quality services. Scott discusses how assessment is used in TQM to measure quality from a customer or stakeholder perspective and compares these uses to traditional uses of assessment.

In Chapter Seven, Curt Kochner and Timothy R. McMahon focus on aspects of organizational development that TQM does not address, including leadership, vision, purpose, organizational culture, motivation, and change. The concept of the learning organization is offered as a model that provides a needed link between the leadership and management discussions.

In Chapter Eight, I present an overview of why student affairs professionals must strive for quality and discuss what quality is *not* and why TQM may fail. The chapter outlines questions that should be addressed as student affairs professionals implement a quality system.

William A. Bryan
Editor

WILLIAM A. BRYAN *is professor of special studies at the University of North Carolina at Wilmington. He served as a chief student affairs officer for eighteen years and is former president of the American College Personnel Association.*

Many educators view the application of TQM as elusive and incompatible with the culture of higher education.

What is Total Quality Management?

William A. Bryan

W. Edwards Deming, Joseph M. Juran, and Philip B. Crosby have long been considered major contributors to the total quality management (TQM) movement in the United States; however, their quality principles and approaches have been more readily embraced by Japanese businesses as Japan has sought to be more competitive in the global market. When Deming went to Japan, he entered a world that was ready for help. In higher education, the issue may be whether we feel that institutions are in trouble with respect to how they provide learning opportunities and services to their students.

Since the late 1980s there has been increasing debate regarding the value of TQM in higher education. Although educators may view TQM as a valuable approach in improving the production of goods, they have not readily embraced basic TQM tenets and principles. Brigham (1994, p. vii) finds that continuous quality improvement (CQI) is the term most commonly used in higher education and states that "CQI is right for higher education provided there is appropriate translation and customization of its principles, proper training and practice, and a bona fide commitment from institutional leaders."

This chapter provides a general overview of TQM and explains why there is pressure for change in higher education institutions. It defines TQM and the various themes, tools, and beliefs that make it different from other management approaches; presents Deming's fourteen principles and how these principles might be applied to student affairs; and provides a discussion of why TQM has become so popular.

Demands on Higher Education

Increasingly, higher education faces criticism by a number of constituencies (customers), all of whom have expectations for improvements to the quality of learning opportunities for students. Public expectations are up and public trust

NEW DIRECTIONS FOR STUDENT SERVICES, no. 76, Winter 1996 © Jossey-Bass Publishers is on the decline. Bogue and Saunders (1992, p. xi) state that "annual media rankings, new accreditation criteria, position statements of regional and national higher education associations, statements of governors, topics of national conferences, frequent book-length critiques of American higher education . . . all point toward an intensified concern for collegiate quality." Lewis and Smith (1994, p. x) state that renewed focus on quality in higher education has occurred because "(1) the environment of higher education is changing and (2) competition for both students and funds will continue to increase, at a time when (3) we are going to have to accomplish more with less." Accomplishing more with less is a theme that generally accompanies the promotion of TQM in higher education. With a changing campus clientele (increased enrollment of women, older, international, minority, and retooling students), higher education faces monumental challenges in serving the needs of a diverse group of customers. Also, a changing knowledge and technology base, a spiraling competitive world market, and funding cuts for needed programs and staff add additional challenges to an already stressed system.

What is TQM?

As I have tried to understand TQM, I have found that the term becomes increasingly elusive. With all that has been written since 1990 about TQM's virtues and curative nature, I assumed that there was an accepted definition of quality and an implementation approach for it. When I believe I have grasped TQM concepts and principles for application in a higher education setting, however, the meaning of TQM slips through my fingers. The following statements provide the reader with a number of perspectives about quality and TQM.

> TQM is a management-driven philosophy that encourages everyone in the organization to know the organizational mission and to adopt a quality philosophy to continuously improve on how the work is done to meet the satisfaction of the customer (Cornesky and McCool, 1992, p. v).
>
> TQM is a comprehensive philosophy of business and management. As such, it can be adopted and put to work only in a carefully planned manner, and over an extended period of time. Full adoption may take anywhere from three years to ten, depending on where the organization is at the beginning of the process (Barrett, 1994, p. 5).
>
> TQM stresses the need for the constant improvement of products and/or services through the involvement of the entire work force. TQM's thrust is process improvement rather than quantity of goods produced. It is a philosophy which views human, technical and engineering subsystems as intertwined through a closely-knit value structure clearly geared to satisfying the customer (Romero-Simpson, 1992, p. 79).
>
> Total Quality is a set of philosophies by which management systems can direct the efficient achievement of the objectives of the organization to

ensure customer satisfaction and maximize stakeholder value. This is accomplished through the continuous improvement of the quality system, which consists of the social system, the technical system, and the management system. Thus, it becomes a way of life for doing business for the entire organization (Lewis and Smith, 1994, p. 29).

It's an approach to management and a set of tools, a coalescing of new and old ideas—from systems thinking and statistical process control, from theories of human behavior, leadership, and planning, plus lessons from earlier, less-than-successful attempts at quality improvement (such as quality circles)—all these brought together in a new orthodoxy (Marchese, 1991, p. 4).

Total quality management (TQM) combines the quality control theory, systems, tools, and organizational models developed over the last forty years in the United States and Japan by W. Edwards Deming, J. M. Juran, and Philip Crosby. TQM is a structured system for creating organization-wide participation in planning and implementing a continuous improvement process. This process should produce results that exceed the expectations of the customer. TQM is built on the assumption that 90 percent of problems are process problems, not employee problems (Coate, 1992, p. 2).

TQM (used interchangeably with the Japanese term TQC) is a *system* for meeting and exceeding customer needs through company-wide continuous improvement based upon the implementation of the Plan-Do-Check-Act Cycle supporting processes, organization, and tools by every manager and employee (GOAL/QPC, 1990, p. 1).

I view TQM in the college setting as being a comprehensive philosophy of operation in which community members (1) are committed to CQI and to a common campus vision, set of values, attitudes, and principles; (2) understand that campus processes need constant review to improve services to customers; (3) believe the work of each community member is vital to customer satisfaction; and (4) value input from customers. For TQM to exist in the campus culture, there must be a commitment to CQI and the training and development of faculty, administration, and staff as a team dedicated to customer service.

After reading the statements on TQM above, most educators would agree that TQM is intentional; sometimes, however, the intent may be seen by some educators as too structured and mechanical. Deming (1986, p. 5) views quality as beginning with intent, "which is fixed by management." Intent is translated by faculty, administration, and staff "into plans, specifications, tests, production" (p. 5). The important point made by Deming is that employees play the pivotal role in implementing quality improvement; therefore, commitment to quality by all players is vital.

Crosby (1979, p. 17) defines quality as "conformance to requirements." With his definition, emphasis is put on intent in TQM and the involvement of all employees in the process. If we talk about quality in student affairs, we must define in specific terms (requirements) how we will measure quality. Is there conformance to our outlined requirements?

Juran (1989) proffers the belief that an agreement on the definition of quality is difficult and that most definitions lack precision. He defines quality as "fitness for use" (p.15), but sees the need to include the words *product* and *customer* when discussing quality. He defines *product* as "the output of any process" (p. 16) and *customer* as "anyone who receives or is affected by the product or process" (p. 17). Therefore, in order for quality to be an issue, there must be a product (goods and services) and a customer (internal or external). From his writings, it is clear that he also sees intent and conformance to requirements as being important elements of quality.

Deming, Crosby, and Juran set the stage for the quality movement in higher education by espousing the importance of quality management to the customer and the worker and by underlining the significance of quality to our future as a country competing in the global marketplace.

TQM Themes

There are many characteristics that describe TQM. It is an organizational struc-ture that

Is not hierarchical
Makes decisions based on facts
Empowers staff to influence and make decisions at the lowest possible level
Engenders the development of trust and commitment as staff work as a team
Seeks data regarding customer needs and expectations and assesses adherence to established standards
Invests in employees by providing opportunities for further staff training and development
Expects managers and supervisors to be leaders who encourage, assist, and facilitate the work of employees
Recognizes the opportunities for CQI in all work functions.

Values. Values are a beginning point in TQM. Barrett (1994) states that "values are the fundamental criteria that people, societies, and organizations use in deciding what is most important to them" (p. 174). The values he sees as basic to TQM are "human dignity, integrity, social responsibilities . . . teams and teamwork, education and training, employee empowerment, continuous improvement . . . change and innovation, and, of course, profitability," to name a few (p. 175). Values determine an organization's behavior, goals, and means of accomplishing priorities. The involvement of community members in the articulation of organization values (Arcaro, 1995a) is an important process in the implementation of TQM and provides for the development of basic oper-ating principles. TQM values customers and is committed to serving and exceeding their expectations; it seeks to understand their changing needs and supports collaborative work teams. As an organizational model, its principles promote a strong belief in the worth and value of people, their ideas and beliefs, and a trust in employees to do the right thing. As noted by Schmidt and Finnigan, TQM seems as if it "demands that we behave on the job in an idealistic fashion. We may not always be able to live up to these expectations, but it's hard to argue with them" (1993, p. 26). TQM values must be stated clearly, and the organization's actions should be reviewed periodically to rectify any inconsistencies.

Mission. There are many definitions of a mission statement: "what business we are in" (Hutton, 1994, p. 113), why we exist (Seymour, 1995), not only what we do but also the customers we serve (Teeter and Lozier, 1993a), and a statement of how a vision will be achieved. A mission statement spells out the purpose of an organization and identifies the constituencies who are served by it. It can be seen as a road map that can be followed to reach an organization's vision—it sets direction and boundaries. Involvement in the formulation and clear understanding of a mission statement by an organization's members is a necessity for TQM to work properly.

Vision. According to Lewis and Smith (1994), vision statements are common beliefs "of what the college or university should be like at some point in the future. An institutional vision is a shared mental image of a desired future—what the college or university wants to be seven to ten years in the future" (p. 120). An organization's vision statement is extremely important in TQM. Generally a vision statement is a reflection of what an organization wants to accomplish, where it wants to go, and what it will be like when its mission and goals are accomplished (Teeter and Lozier, 1993a; Hutton, 1994). It is focused on the future. In TQM, community members are involved in the development of such a statement.

Teams. Teams are a cornerstone of TQM. The characteristics outlined in the preceding paragraphs highlight the importance of teams in implementing basic principles of TQM. They aid in developing a participative atmosphere where employees have a stake in the success of their work. Also, teams provide the setting for developing a culture that values each member's contribution and helps each member to feel connected to and responsible for the organization—"where work is fun and morale is high" (Cornesky and McCool, 1994, p. 5). There can be many teams with differing functions: teams that focus on department or division process problems, planning, or review of professional standards, to name a few. Scholtes (1993) provides excellent coverage of teams and their importance in TQM.

Customers. The customer is paramount in TQM (Harris and Baggett, 1992). Although higher education institutions are service organizations, the term *customer* has met with some resistance. Nevertheless, it is well understood by student affairs professionals, who have always seen the primary goal of their work as serving the needs of their customers. The key question may be, "Is the customer always right?" As Roberts points out, students have limits to their empowerment; there are ground rules to which they must adhere.

"Empowerment does not imply an immediate adoption of all suggestions from students" (1995, p. 85). Student views must be taken seriously; there will always be differing perspectives, styles, and values. The conflict is how student affairs professionals see their educational function. We are concerned with student learning and development; we are teachers in a nontraditional setting. We serve diverse customers with varying expectations. We strive to recruit, satisfy, and retain our customers. Our priority must be knowing as much as possible about who we serve and meeting or exceeding their expectations.

Shared Leadership. Possibly the key element in the success of TQM is shared leadership. Arcaro (1995a) puts it this way: "Management must 'walk the talk.' Management must preach and practice the quality principles" (p. 64). Managers must clearly chart the vision and mission of the enterprise shared and supported by all participants. In TQM all participants are, as Barrett says, "expected to exercise leadership whenever the situation is appropriate" (1994, p. 99). Teams are vital to the achievement of TQM and they have a special responsibility to enhance member leadership skills through special training programs.

Continuous Improvement. A basic tenet of TQM is that any process "can and should be improved" (Lewis and Smith, 1994, p. 14); therefore, all processes and systems are continuously reviewed and revised when change in customer expectations or needs is identified. This tenet suggests a commitment to continuously improving ways of doing work and, as Lewis and Smith observe, "involves searching unceasingly for ever-higher levels of quality by isolating sources of defects" (p. 315). Continuous improvement is often defined as the ultimate goal of a TQM organization.

Process. Throughout the literature on TQM, process is identified as being important to quality improvement. Juran defines process as "a systematic series of actions directed to the achievement of a goal" (1988, p. 169); Seymour defines it as "a method for doing things" (1995, p. 32). Further, Seymour states that "an organization is only as effective as its processes and systems" (p. 32). When a problem is identified, rather than focusing on an individual as the cause of the problem, the focus is on a process or set of processes. In TQM, every step in a process adds worth to the total delivery of a quality service.

Information. Barrett states that "achieving a high level of excellence in . . . information management capabilities is one of the prime objectives of TQM" (1994, p. 94). Accurate, timely information is indispensable to any organization. In a TQM organization, information must be free-flowing, and needed data and facts must be intentionally gathered and analyzed for impact on both processes and delivery of quality services to customers. The development of an information system that provides accurate, timely data for planning greatly affects change in any organization. Seeking opinions from customers and assessing the quality of services is necessary for an organization to continuously improve—to the delight of its customers.

Professional Development. Student affairs professionals provide the human capital necessary for TQM to be successful. "If you expect people to change the way they do things," writes Arcaro, "you must provide them with the tools necessary to change their work processes. Training provides people with the tools necessary to improve their work processes" (1995a, p. 64). For professional development to be effective, supervisors and staff must participate in a two-way process that identifies staff interests and needs and strengthens leadership's commitment to educating staff so that consumers are provided with quality services. A means of accomplishing this might be the formation of a professional development committee that meets the needs of management and support staff.

Empowerment. Meaningful decision making at the lowest possible organizational level is basic to TQM. Empowerment means encouraging people "to be open, creative, and innovative in finding new ways of working to achieve their vision" (Arcaro, 1995a, p. 14). Basic to this concept is the commitment of managers and leaders to the professional development and involvement of their staff; this commitment mandates specific educational efforts and training and the encouragement of risk taking. Employees are encouraged to make their own decisions, set their own work standards and goals, organize their work, and deal directly with customers (Barrett, 1994).

TQM Tools

Ewell (1992) believes that a longitudinal student database is an important tool for managing quality in higher education. Accurate data and information are critical requirements for TQM. The general themes of TQM consistently point to the importance of teamwork and collaboration; data and good communications for decisions; management's commitment to listening, studying, and implementing needed changes; and the use of basic statistical tools and scientific approaches.

Leadership must use a variety of tools to ensure quality. The most commonly used tools in TQM include affinity diagrams, brainstorming, cause-and-effect diagrams (fishbone diagrams), checksheets or checklists, control charts, dot-plot and stem-and-leaf displays, flowcharts, forcefield analyses, histograms, multivoting, nominal group techniques, operational definitions, Pareto diagrams, relations diagrams, run charts, scattergrams, spreadsheets, stratification and is–is-not analyses, systematic diagrams, and time plots (Arcaro, 1995b; Cornesky and McCool, 1994; GOAL/QPC,1990; Juran, 1988; Seymour, 1995; Sherr and Teeter, 1991; Scholtes, 1993). When there is training in the appropriate use and application of these tools, they are powerful aids to reaching quality. Organizations should not become enamored with drawing perfect flowcharts or fishbone diagrams, however. These tools are not "an end in themselves," as Lozier and Teeter point out, but rather "a means to process improvement" (1993b, p. 130) and good communication. Unfortunately, some organizations "adopt a standardized, lockstep TQM program in which tool A is always used when performing step 1" (Lozier and Teeter, 1993b, p. 130) without considering the organization's uniqueness, work climate, and culture.

Applying Deming's Fourteen Principles to Student Affairs

Deming's (1986) principles can help any organization develop a quality culture. They can equally apply to a division of student affairs; although, in the application of these principles, campus culture and political climate and the uniqueness and culture of a student affairs division must be assessed. What follows is a statement of each of Deming's principles (1986) and a restatement of each principle for the student affairs environment.

PRINCIPLE 1: *Create constancy of purpose toward improvement of product and service, with the aim to become competitive and to stay in business, and to provide jobs (p. 23).*

   Create a constancy of purpose toward improvement of services and programs. The aim is to create quality student learning, development, and services for student success on campus and in their future communities. Vision, mission, and goal statements that are clear and that have achievable and measurable objectives are imperative, as are strategies to accomplish goals. The development of these statements should include staff, faculty, students, and administrators. Although many student affairs staff focus on the learning and educational nature of their jobs, there is a need to emphasize that the services and programs they provide are necessary and are provided at a reasonable cost.

PRINCIPLE 2: *Adopt the new philosophy. We are in a new economic age. Western management must awaken to the challenge, must learn their responsibilities, and take on leadership for change (p. 23).*

   Adopt a continuous improvement philosophy. Staff must adopt a philosophy of continuous improvement that exceeds customer expectations. They must learn new skills, be leaders in different settings, and accept a shared responsibility for the enhancement of student learning, development, and services. Higher education is facing new social and economic challenges. Student affairs professionals must be responsive to a changing student population with diverse learning modes and to the demands of external constituencies. Staff must recognize the new challenges and responsibilities that these diverse constituencies bring to the campus and must provide leadership for effective and productive change.

PRINCIPLE 3: *Cease dependence on inspection to achieve quality. Eliminate the need for inspection on a mass basis by building quality into the product in the first place (p. 23).*

Build quality into processes from the beginning. Customer-focused programs and activities that meet or exceed goals and standards and ongoing process evaluation are all key elements to quality assurance. Develop a culture in which staff constantly seek new avenues to improve service. Partnering and teamwork are necessary to provide quality processes.

PRINCIPLE 4: *End the practice of awarding business on the basis of price tag. Instead, minimize total cost. Move toward a single supplier for any one item, on a long-term relationship of loyalty and trust (p. 23).*

Develop productive relationships with parents, school educators, and students. Work closely with feeder institutions, parents, and prospective students to improve the quality of students entering higher education. Relationships can be nurtured from the first parent-student contact with the institution and further enhanced through parent involvement in various university activities. High school and community college educators can be helpful in improving university student transfer, course articulation, and curriculum design processes. Communication with internal and external constituencies is key to improving quality. Building long-term relationships that invite inclusiveness and recognize legitimate contributions to the work of student affairs professionals will encourage the development of trust.

PRINCIPLE 5: *Improve constantly and forever the system of production and service, to improve quality and productivity, and thus constantly decrease costs (p. 23).*

Improve continuously the ways in which students and other customers are served. The tools identified previously can be aids to improving quality. Identify quality variances and needed improvements, propose changes, implement changes, evaluate success of changes, and adjust processes to improve quality. Listen to customers. This is a never-ending cycle.

PRINCIPLE 6: *Institute training on the job (p. 23).*

Institute training and development activities and programs for professional, support, and student staff. All individuals working within a student affairs division should be included in the provision of programs and activities that meet needs for quality service and professional and personal growth. These activities and programs can promote knowledge about TQM tools, open communication, understanding, and trust. They further the development of good morale and of a culture that truly serves and is committed to the development of human capital.

PRINCIPLE 7: *Institute leadership. . . . The aim of supervision should be to help people and machines and gadgets to do a better job. Supervision of management is in need of overhaul, as well as supervision of production workers (p. 23).*

Initiate educational leadership. Management must develop an open and supportive atmosphere that provides initiative and direction and encourages staff to assume leadership at the lowest possible level. The development of a vision, mission, and goal statement by staff, faculty, and students should be a shared process that promotes teamwork. Management must "walk the talk."

PRINCIPLE 8: *Drive out fear, so that everyone may work effectively for the company (p. 23).*

Eliminate fear. Drive fear from the workplace. Promote an environment where all community members feel free to express their views, have no fear of failure or ridicule, and feel empowered to make decisions. Promote a climate that encourages open debate where differences of opinion are encouraged in the pursuit of excellence.

PRINCIPLE 9: *Break down barriers between departments. People in research, design, sales, and production must work as a team, to foresee problems of production and in use that may be encountered with the product or service (p. 24).*

Eliminate barriers to excellence. Leadership is responsible for promoting a community where all are valued for their work and its importance in meeting the unit's mission. Cross-functional work teams promote collaboration instead of competition and a broader understanding of student affairs functions. Poor communication is a major barrier. When barriers are removed, change is welcomed and not feared.

PRINCIPLE 10: *Eliminate slogans, exhortations, and targets for the work force asking for zero defects and new levels of productivity. Such exhortations only create adversarial relationships, as the bulk of the causes of low quality and low productivity belong to the system and thus lie beyond the power of the work force (p. 24).*

Develop a quality culture. In most cases, problems are not created by people but by processes. Everyone is involved in a quality culture and quality is everyone's responsibility. A quality culture depends on all community members assuming leadership in finding solutions to problems. Empowerment of each community member, open communication, and attitudes of teamwork and excellence contribute to a quality culture. Slogans and exhortations are directed at the wrong people.

PRINCIPLE 11: *Eliminate work standards (quotas) on the factory floor. Eliminate management by objective. Eliminate management by numbers, numerical goals. Substitute leadership (p. 24).*

Eliminate numerical objectives and quotas. The establishment of numerical objectives and quotas does not contribute to quality improvement. Increased programming does not equal quality. Focus the organization's work on providing leadership to improve processes so that students have quality educational experiences.

PRINCIPLE 12: *Remove barriers that rob the hourly worker of his right to pride of workmanship. The responsibility of supervisors must be changed from sheer numbers to quality. Remove barriers that rob people in management and in engineering of their right to pride of workmanship. This means,* inter alia, *abolishment of the annual or merit rating and of management by objective (p. 24).*

Remove barriers that hinder people in taking pride in their work or in being creative. Leadership has a basic belief that people want to be involved in their work and take pride in a job well done. Staff are encouraged to interact as professionals collaborating to provide quality service and to individually identify professional and personal growth objectives. The work culture must promote empowerment and engender in each person a sense of ownership of the organization's work.

PRINCIPLE 13: *Institute a vigorous program of education and self-improvement (p. 24).*

Institute a comprehensive program of professional development, education, and personal development. Basic to the continuous pursuit of quality is the development of programs and activities that improve staff work skills and further their understanding of vision and mission for an organization; the support of staff involvement in student affairs activities is also crucial. Further, staff should be encouraged and supported by leadership to be involved in continuing education and personal development programs.

PRINCIPLE 14: *Put everybody in the company to work to accomplish the transformation. The transformation is everybody's job (p. 24).*

Encourage a culture in which staff accept responsibility for achieving excellence (implementing the prior thirteen principles each day). Quality of services and programs is everyone's job. The implementation of quality principles requires commitment from all staff. Quality occurs incrementally every day. Each staff member is unique and has specific skills to contribute to accomplishing the organization's vision and mission.

To employ these principles, all staff must be committed to a common student affairs philosophy and body of knowledge about what constitutes quality student affairs practice. The development of a vision and mission statement provide direction for an organization as it puts into practice its commitment to continuous improvement. A customer focus with a communication link to feeder institutions, parents, and prospective students is at the heart of improving quality. Staff need training and development, an open and supportive atmosphere, and freedom to express views without ridicule in order for quality leadership to flourish. Important in providing a strong foundation for a quality culture, however, is the development of a sense of community that values everyone's contribution, trusts people to do the right thing, understands that problems stem from faulty processes—not faulty people, and understands that quality is everyone's responsibility.

Why Has TQM Become Popular?

As higher education moves into the twenty-first century, it is faced with an accelerating rate of growth of new information, knowledge, and change as new demands are made on its systems. Some educators believe that quality already exists within the confines of their campuses and that little can be gained from the business principles of TQM. As educators are increasingly exposed to the principles and practices associated with TQM, however, they find a quality framework compatible with "the best existing practices in higher education" (Lewis and Smith, 1994, p. 6). TQM views the dynamics of actions in the environment as offering opportunities for change and not as threats to the existence of an organization. Today, as in business, higher education leaders are facing new challenges from the public sector and competition among institutions; they seek a competitive edge as they recruit and serve students.

Facing budget cuts and demands to provide more services with less money and human resources, educators are also looking for new ways to conduct their traditional responsibilities. Educators may see TQM as the imposition of new management principles, but TQM promotes many powerful approaches and well-accepted philosophies of doing business in which the customer is the main focus. TQM in higher education is calling for a reexamination of the core values we endorse as we conduct business. An academic system with a strong set of values and operating principles will be better able to chart its course in a sea of constant change. As Arcaro posits, "TQM unites an organization; it pulls together the collective resources of the organization to focus on developing creative ideas to solve today's problems" (Arcaro, 1995b, pp. 1–2).

Perhaps TQM is becoming more popular because it allows a quick response to customer needs, collects information and data to better focus limited resources to meet customer needs, promotes problem solving for systematic improvement, encourages organization members to use their skills and abilities, and is continuously focused on improving processes (Roberts, 1995). These potential results warrant a closer study of the value of TQM in higher education and its total system approach.

References

Arcaro, J. S. *Quality in Education: An Implementation Handbook.* Delray Beach, Fla.: St. Lucie Press, 1995a.

Arcaro, J. S. *Teams in Education: Creating an Integrated Approach.* Delray-Beach, Fla.: St. Lucie Press, 1995b.

Barrett, D. *Fast Focus on TQM: A Concise Guide to Companywide Learning.* Portland, Oreg.: Productivity Press, 1994.

Bogue, E. G., and Saunders, R. L. *The Evidence for Quality: Strengthening the Tests of Academic and Administrative Effectiveness.* San Francisco: Jossey-Bass, 1992.

Brigham, S. "Introduction." In *AAHE Continuous Quality Improvement Project, CUI 101: A First Reader for Higher Education.* Washington, D.C.: American Association for Higher Education, 1994.

Coate, L. E. *Total Quality Management at Oregon State University.* Washington, D.C.: National Association of College and University Business Officers, 1992.

Cornesky, R., and McCool, S. *Total Quality Improvement Guide for Institutions of Higher Education.* (2nd ed.). Madison, Wis.: Magna, 1994.

Crosby, P. B. *Quality Is Free.* New York: McGraw-Hill, 1979.

Deming, W. E. *Out of the Crisis.* Cambridge, Mass.: MIT Center for Advanced Engineering Study, 1986.

Ewell, P. T. "Longitudinal Student Databases: A Critical Tool for Managing Quality in Higher Education." In J. W. Harris and J. M. Baggett (eds.), *Quality Quest in the Academic Process.* Birmingham, Ala.: Samford University, 1992.

GOAL/QPC. *Hoshin Planning: A Planning System for Implementing Total Quality Management (TQM).* GOAL/QPC Research Committee, 1989 Research Report no. 89–10–03. Methuen, Mass.: GOAL/QPC, 1990.

Harris, J. W., and Baggett, J. M. *Quality Quest in the Academic Process.* Birmingham, Ala.: Samford University, 1992.

Hutton, D. W. *The Change Agent's Handbook.* Milwaukee, Wis.: ASQC Quality Press, 1994.

Juran, J. M. *Juran on Planning for Quality.* New York: Free Press, 1988.

Juran, J. M. *Juran on Leadership for Quality.* New York: Free Press, 1989.

Lewis, R. G., and Smith, D. H. *Total Quality in Higher Education.* Delray Beach, Fla.: St. Lucie Press, 1994.

Lozier, G. G., and Teeter, D. J. "The Challenge: Overcoming the Pitfalls." In D. J. Teeter and G. G. Lozier (eds.), *Pursuit of Quality in Higher Education: Case Studies in Total Quality Management.* New Directions for Student Services, no. 78. San Francisco: Jossey-Bass, 1993a.

Lozier, G. G., and Teeter, D. J. "Six Foundations of Total Quality Management." In D. J. Teeter and G. G. Lozier (eds.), *Pursuit of Quality in Higher Education: Case Studies in Total Quality Management.* New Directions for Student Services, no. 78. San Francisco: Jossey-Bass, 1993b.

Marchese, T. "TQM Reaches the Academy." *AAHE Bulletin,* Nov. 1991, pp. 3–9.

Roberts, H. V. *Academic Initiatives in Total Quality for Higher Education.* Milwaukee, Wis.: ASQC Quality Press, 1995.

Romero-Simpson, J. E. "A Total Quality Management (TQM) Organizational Behavior Course." In J. W. Harris and J. M. Baggett (eds.), *Quality Quest in the Academic Process.* Birmingham, Ala.: Samford University, 1992.

Scholtes, P. R. *The Team Handbook.* Madison, Wis.: Joiner, 1993.

Seymour, D. *Once Upon a Campus.* Phoenix, Ariz.: American Council on Education and Oryx Press, 1995.

Sherr, L. A., and Teeter, D. J. (eds.). *Total Quality Management in Higher Education.* New Directions for Student Services, no. 71. San Francisco: Jossey-Bass, 1991.

WILLIAM A. BRYAN *is professor of specialty studies at the University of North Carolina at Wilmington. He served as a chief student affairs officer for eighteen years and is a former president of the American College Personnel Association.*

Student affairs leaders should evaluate the negatives as well as the positives of implementing TQM.

Pros and Cons of TQM for Student Affairs

Nancy Lee Howard

Colleges and universities continue to search for ways to best manage the complexities facing academic organizations. This search has led many institutions to experiment with total quality management (TQM). In this chapter, key benefits and costs of implementing TQM in student affairs are identified. The realities—negative and positive—are examined first through the experiences of early innovators and second using the Baldrige criteria (explained further below). Early innovators have employed a myriad of approaches. In 1993, eighteen colleges and universities formed the Academic Quality Consortium (AQC) around a shared belief that the applicability of TQM to higher education should be explored (Seymour, 1996). AQC institutions and others have implemented TQM in various areas, including student affairs. The experiences of these pioneers and others enable us to explore the efficacy of TQM.

The Malcolm Baldrige National Quality Award (MBNQA) presents a second way to assess the effectiveness of TQM. Created in 1987 through federal legislation, the MBNQA established criteria to evaluate excellence in business and industry. The purposes of the Baldrige Award are to promote awareness of the importance of quality improvement to the national economy; to recognize organizations that have made substantial improvements in products, services, and overall competitive performance; and to foster sharing of best-practices information among U.S. organizations (National Institute of Standards and Technology, 1995, p. 1). In 1995, pilot criteria were introduced to assess specifically educational organizations. The MBNQA criteria paint a picture of what high performance looks like once achieved. High performance is defined as approaching work tasks and activities systematically. The goal is to achieve ever-higher levels of overall performance (National Institute, 1996). Education pilot criteria are as follows: leadership, information and analysis, strategic and operational planning, human resource development and management, educational and business process management, school performance results, and student focus and student and stakeholder satisfaction (National Institute, 1995). The goal of the MBNQA framework is the delivery of ever-improving educational services that lead to student success and satisfaction (National Institute, 1995). We can also thereby assess the pros and cons of TQM in relation to how it moves student affairs toward a level of high performance resulting in student success and satisfaction.

Pros

Many benefits can arise from implementing TQM. In this section, several potential positive outcomes are discussed.

Stakeholder Value Through Customer Focus. An important tenet of TQM is customer focus. Empirical evidence suggests that customer focus alone may be more important than implementing TQM (Powell, 1995). According to the MBNQA criteria, high-performing organizations determine near-term and longer-term requirements and expectations of customers. Interactions and relationships with customers are effectively managed and trends and current levels of customer satisfaction and dissatisfaction are monitored. Customer satisfaction compares favorably with appropriate benchmarks and competing services (National Institute, 1995).

In TQM, a customer is broadly defined as whoever receives the services of the organization. An important step toward high performance is for all people in an organization to acknowledge that they are employed to provide a service to someone else: their customers. Current thinking in business and industry has focused on "return on quality"—making sure that the quality offered is the same quality that customers want. If business and industry's experience applies to colleges and universities, it is vital that a clear focus on customer wants and needs be maintained. Otherwise, efforts to pursue high performance are not only unnecessarily costly but also ineffective (Greising, 1994).

Higher education has a history of assuming that it knows what is best for customers. One exception is student affairs, which is dedicated to serving its customers—students. The philosophy of serving customers fits well with the objectives and motivations of student affairs professionals; it is natural for them to initiate plans focused on meeting student wants and needs. It is not uncommon to survey students and gather information about how best to meet their expectations. Total quality management provides structure, direction, and support to student affairs activities aimed at gathering student feedback. Further, TQM integrates student feedback into broader plans and activities.

An example of TQM application in the admissions office at Oregon State University is presented below (C. Torset, personal communication, May 7, 1992).

Quality in Action: Improving the Admissions Application Process. The Office of Admissions established a TQM team to review the incoming mail process and telephone reception operation. Their goal was to provide a higher level of service to admissions applicants. After initial team formation, the operational review was expanded to encompass the entire mail and telephone operations processes. The team's issue statement read, "Model the material flow to better fit the BANNER student information system, thereby increasing the efficiency of the admissions process." A number of steps were included in their review.

1. *Process review.* After creating a process flowchart of the tasks currently performed by personnel in the mail-phone area, it was apparent that ways to streamline the mail process included: (a) identifying the steps necessary for the entry of information into the BANNER system and (b) creating a new flow process that would allow for efficient, accurate, and consistent data entry.

To achieve such improvement, it was necessary to de-couple the mail process from other tasks. The mail process steps were broken down into simple procedures that could be repetitively performed, thereby promoting greater efficiency without negatively impacting other essential operations (such as answering phone calls). The team's analysis (a simplified time and motion study) illuminated potential solutions.

2. *Cause analysis.* A review of the process flowchart revealed the mail processing operation was designed prior to the advent of computer support. Many operations required previously, such as alphabetizing incoming mail, were no longer necessary with BANNER. However, as the staff was learning the new student information system they were still using the old operating procedures.

3. *Data collection.* Data were collected by evaluating three distinct aspects of the internal operations, as well as by analyzing three surveys designed to identify the needs of external users. Survey results supported team members' hunches about user expectations: accurate and timely evaluation of applications; timely communication of an admission decision; prompt replies to requests for information; and inquiries via telephone answered with courtesy, accuracy, and professionalism.

The data collected on operations (automated call distributor statistics, application processing time, and mail folder processing time) provided clear, unrefutable evidence that the current operation was not meeting the needs and expectations of the clients.

4. *Solutions.* First, critical process steps were identified. They included opening mail and rough sorting, data entry into BANNER, file creation, material collection, and delivery to evaluation staff. Next the TQM team developed

operating procedures, position requirements, and job descriptions. In addition to team members' own ideas, the solutions incorporated lessons learned from benchmarking sister-institution admissions operations. Technology improvements were implemented, including enhancing the effectiveness of the automated call distributor system. Personnel responsibilities were redefined and associated changes were implemented. Specific processes were physically relocated to more appropriate work spaces.

5. *Results.* Proposed solutions were approved and fully supported by senior administration. Operational efficiencies were immediately achieved. The most significant result was the reduction of the average turnaround time for freshman application processing from sixty-seven days to eleven days.

Employee Commitment and Development Through Involvement. TQM is a commitment to excellence by each person in the organization. Excellence is achieved by teamwork and a dedication to being the best through delivery of high-quality services that exceed the expectations of customers. As with any significant cultural change, TQM requires employees at many different levels to participate in leadership behavior. This presents a tremendous opportunity for employee growth and development. Inspiring people to work differently demands the ability to communicate clearly what needs to be done and why. Having a clear goal or vision, imparting that vision to others, and demonstrating personal commitment through actions directed at making the vision a reality are the foundations of TQM leadership.

TQM requires leadership actions that empower people to achieve a shared vision of organizational purpose and direction. The quality of the work being done then becomes the responsibility of all employees who express ownership through pride in their results, teamwork, and commitment to customers. No college or university has successfully implemented and maintained progress with TQM without employee empowerment. One significant advantage to TQM is that it gives employees a voice (Seymour, 1991).

High-performance MBNQA organizations enable the entire workforce to develop its full potential to pursue the organization's quality and operational performance objectives. An environment for quality excellence conducive to full participation, as well as personal and organizational growth, can be built and maintained through TQM. MBNQA criteria endorse treating education and training as integral human resources functions. Further, employee performance, recognition, promotion, compensation, reward, and feedback approaches support the improvement of quality and operational performance (National Institute, 1995).

Next, an example of employee commitment and development being enhanced through TQM is presented (M. Henthorne, personal communication, May 7, 1992).

Quality in Action: Improving the Student Union Building Services. The student-union staff set about creating cultural change using TQM and systems-thinking approaches. Their stated purpose was to strive toward continuous process improvement through systems thinking. They believed it was possible to draw on every employee's intellect and creativity by using systems thinking (Henthorne, 1993). Using Peter Senge's book, *The Fifth Discipline*, (1992) as a guide, the team agreed to follow the basic tenets of systems thinking: support one another; tell the truth (people usually do, but due to a lack of trust, they often only tell half the story); continually be in an inquiry mode; know that nobody knows everything and everyone can learn; and finally, a mistake is not the real problem—it's how we look at a mistake that is the problem.

Further, the team identified specific cultural changes they hoped to achieve:

From	*Toward*
Solve the problem	Help one another learn
Form a task force	Involve everyone
Find a better technique	Identify a valued purpose
Do it all right now	Do what is "do-able" in reality

The team created a shared vision: to increase the level of satisfaction and comfort felt by casual users of the Memorial Union (MU) and persons planning and attending events held in the MU. To achieve their vision, the team increased the level of communication among the members of the team responsible for preparation of the MU for daily use and for special events in it. Further, they practiced the tenets of systems thinking in their team meetings and in executing individual tasks. Examples of systems thinking began to show up in new projects. One project resulted in a new training session and resource materials designed to teach student organization leaders how to present productions in the MU ballroom using television broadcast management procedures.

Team members were asked to comment on their experience with systems thinking. Their comments included: "It helps me to understand the other employees' perspectives." "It gets me to focus on the customers' likes, dislikes, and needs as I go about my daily tasks." "It gives the department a greater level of consistency in services and presents a unified image of who we are and what we can do well." "It builds respect for other parts of the process." "It brings people together who share common tasks but may work in different buildings or work various times and days of the week."

Service Betterment Through Continuous Process Improvement. Volumes of anecdotal evidence assert TQM results in improved products and services (see Brigham, 1994a; Harris and Baggett, 1992; Roberts, 1995; Walton, 1986). Service and product improvement ensues when work processes are improved. Using a problem-solving model together with quality tools provides a systematic, objective way to examine and improve work processes. Figure 2.1 illustrates one example of a problem-solving process.

Figure 2.1. Oregon State University Problem-Solving Model

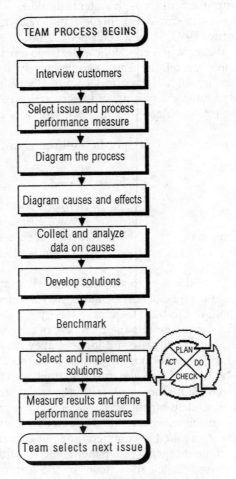

In many organizations, one quickly discovers that quite often very little thought goes into process design. Instead, the focus is on getting the job done as opposed to determining how to do the job most effectively. Rarely do we allow ourselves the luxury of taking time out from actually doing the work to evaluate how we do the work. Colleges and universities, however, are finding that employee involvement in process improvements focused on customer needs and wants is an important first step toward high performance.

Student affairs comprises numerous processes. Every process entails a series of steps. Nearly every student affairs process is worthy of study using TQM tools. The following list is a sample of student affairs processes that could be reviewed using TQM tools.

Function	Process
Enrollment management	Recruitment and marketing
	Admissions
	Financial aid delivery
	Scholarship management
	New student orientation
	Retention
	Advising
	Development of course schedule
	Registration
	Records maintenance
	Transcripting
	Enrollment verification
	Graduation
Housing and residence programs	Facilities management
	Residence life management
Financial aid	Student aid delivery
	Data collection and reporting
	Scholarship management
	Student aid coordination
Student support services	Academic support
	Student life support
	Instruction and advising
Student health services	Patient education
	Health promotion
	Disease prevention
	Diagnosis
	Treatment
Career services	Employer recruitment
	Work experience
	Information delivery and marketing
	Training and education
Food service delivery	Purchasing
	Inventory management
	Production
	Education
	Program support
Educational activities	Retail goods and service delivery
	Events management
	Recreational sports administration
Shared or similar generic processes	Receipt and review of applications
	Fiscal management
	Administration
	Facilities management

TQM promotes high performance by its focus on service-product-process improvement. In MBNQA high-performance organizations, work processes are managed. Process management includes design of new processes, management of day-to-day activities, improvement of quality and operational performance, and assessment of quality. All work units, including suppliers, contribute to overall quality and operational performance requirements. Processes are continuously improved (National Institute, 1995).

An example of service betterment through continuous process improvement is given in the next section (R. Martinez, personal communication, May 7, 1992).

Quality in Action: Improving the Financial Aid Process. The financial aid office formed a TQM team to address customer concerns. Specifically, students wanted to receive their financial aid funds at the beginning of each Fall term. Further, customers felt the process was taking too long, especially considering that they had provided requested information months in advance.

A student survey provided additional information that aided staff in better understanding customer expectations. Student concerns included receiving aid on time; treatment received when seeking service; staff being helpful with questions; being notified of financial aid award in a timely manner; the office not losing submitted materials; and follow-through with initial award after file was completed.

The team agreed on the following issue statement: "Reduce the number of days from receipt of on-time financial aid applications through the verification process." The process was flowcharted and reviewed, then streamlined. Tasks and services were prioritized. The teams' effort resulted in reducing the average turnaround time from 44 days to 3 days.

Reduced Costs Through Elimination of Unnecessary Tasks. As in many organizations, student affairs professionals will hear upper management trumpeting the necessity of "doing more with less." However, a more realistic result of implementing TQM is doing less with less. TQM practices enable organizations to ferret out and eliminate unnecessary activities (waste and rework). Cost savings are recognized when activities are done once (and done correctly); work processes are simplified to require less staff time (unnecessary steps are eliminated; levels of review and required signatures are reduced); and duplicate parallel structures and processes (that is, shadow systems) are eliminated.

Financial savings through reduced costs are a significant benefit of TQM. Using TQM tools and approaches can result in reducing the costs associated with an ongoing activity. For example, if the admissions application review process is simplified and streamlined, the cost of completing the process will be reduced. Even greater cost savings result when costs are not accrued in the first place. For example, if housing application deposits are routinely refunded when prospective students enroll elsewhere, eliminating the deposit process entirely might be advantageous. Finally, it's important to note that at least one journalist goes further and suggests that quality initiatives not only can reduce costs, but must reduce costs in order to justify the cost of implementing quality initiatives (Greising, 1994).

Better Decisions Through Use of Fact and Data. MBNQA high-performance organizations use data and information to maintain a customer focus, to drive quality excellence, and to improve operational performance (National Institute, 1995). Decision making based on fact and data is an important premise of TQM; although this makes intuitive sense, it is admittedly challenging to identify appropriate outcome measures for higher education. Further, employees get caught in the cycle of doing the work and find it difficult to take time out to measure what is done. Yet identifying what information is necessary for effective decision making is a valuable benefit of TQM. TQM provides a basis for sorting and responding to competing demands. It helps a unit identify performance and outcome measures that link to organization goals. Instead of focusing on the quantity of activity alone, TQM encourages attention to process and results. Further, TQM helps student affairs professionals define the most significant quality measures.

TQM encourages employees to question whether events are common or special causes. It demands that rather than jumping to a solution, student affairs professionals must instead ask the following questions: Do we have, as Teeter asks, the data to support "the position we are taking on this issue and has the issue been systematically studied" (1994, p. 4). Thoughtful effort at the outset results in better decisions in the end.

Goal Achievement Through Strategic Planning. In MBNQA high-performance organizations, key quality and operational performance requirements are integrated into overall organization planning. Specific quality and operational performance plans exist for the short term and longer term. Plan requirements are deployed to all work units (National Institute, 1995). TQM strategic quality planning efforts build upon a university's existing strategic planning process. With TQM, formal strategic planning is conducted; adjustments and modifications occur frequently. A successful student affairs unit must know where it is headed and how it plans to get there; TQM can help make this happen.

Flexibility Through Portability to Individual Units. Although there is no single, commonly accepted definition of TQM, most definitions emphasize widespread, extensive involvement from everyone in the organization (Eskildson, 1995). The concepts can definitely be used in individual student affairs departments, however, even if the entire institution does not embrace TQM.

Cons

It is important to evaluate the arguments against TQM. Thoughtful consideration of the cons can lead to selecting implementation strategies that mitigate potential negative consequences.

Costs Associated with Resistance. Addressing resistance to change is a major obstacle to implementing TQM. Many people in an organization have difficulty seeing why change of any type, let alone change through TQM, is necessary. Some resist change itself, whereas others resist the perception of being changed. Fear of the unknown can be overwhelming. Resistance is encountered when the need for specific change is not apparent to those affected by the changes or those who are asked to interface with or implement changes. Frequently, TQM is seen as added work. Further, some staff fail to see how their efforts will make a difference or feel quality improvement is not rewarded by the organization. Others feel that the larger system demands suboptimization, and therefore local efforts to improve quality are largely pointless. Another source of resistance is due to fear of loss of control (Brigham, 1994b).

Resistance takes many shapes and forms, and can result in a tremendous drain of resources and energy. Resistance to TQM can occur right at the outset, when initial training sessions are scheduled. For example, employees resist TQM training by refusing to attend (announcing they are too busy); not showing up; attending, but not participating; criticizing the training; failing to use the training in the workplace; or refusing to allow subordinate employees to attend training (Peachy, 1994).

Resistance can crop up among student affairs leaders as well. Leaders resist taking responsibility for implementing TQM by proclaiming that TQM is just the latest management fad; continuing to execute authoritarian behavior; paying lip service to TQM by outwardly promoting it but providing no follow-through or support; refusing to implement employee suggestions; and failing to recognize employee contributions (Peachy, 1994).

Organizational change is confronted with less resistance when people who must accept and implement change have been involved from the outset in bringing about the change. Unfortunately, student affairs professionals may be tempted to implement TQM through top-down edicts. They and others will discover that to successfully implement TQM requires an inclusive implementation plan that directly addresses dealing with resistance. Clearly, some student affairs leaders may determine the negatives of dealing with resistance in their organization, along with the associated energy drain, may outweigh the benefits that might be achieved through TQM.

Tendency to Focus on Internal Processes Rather Than External Customers and Results. MBNQA high-performance organizations accomplish effective outcomes as measured by achievement levels and trends in quality, organizational operational performance, and supplier quality. In successful organizations, current quality and operational performance levels compare favorably with appropriate benchmarks and competing services (National Institute, 1995). It is difficult to measure outputs in colleges and universities, however. When does one know student learning has occurred? How does one know whether focusing on student life experiences has benefited the greater community?

Student affairs professionals may find it easier to avoid such difficult questions and focus on internal process improvements. Yet successful TQM initiatives must cultivate closer customer relationships and grapple with difficult customer issues. Determining and meeting customer requirements is essential. Unfortunately, doing so is quite difficult.

A related challenge is the difficulty that some faculty and staff have in designating students as customers. Some educators argue that students do not know what is best for them, or that students are not customers (although this is less the attitude among student affairs professionals than among other college and university staff). Further, student affairs is part of a larger organization with multiple customers competing for limited resources. Grappling with the customer concept alone is difficult. The higher education customer base changes constantly—students come and go not only every year but every term. Also, depending on how they are categorized (domestic, international, older-than-average, etc.), students have different needs, wants, and expectations. Again, some student affairs leaders might choose not to pursue TQM because of these challenges.

Costs Associated with Time and Resource Commitment. Pursuing TQM requires commitment of time and resources. The issue of time is an overwhelming frustration faced by practitioners (Seymour, 1991). It takes time to learn about TQM and to apply TQM concepts. Especially during initial implementation, when training needs are high, TQM takes staff time away from their normal workloads. This can result in a significant burden on student affairs, which is often leanly budgeted. Employees may feel that they do not have time to learn new ways of doing things or do not have the extra time to apply quality practices through team-based activities. Often, student affairs employees find themselves pulled between their primary concern—working with students—and the need to participate in TQM activities. Although it is not intended to be, some employees will see these two sets of demands as mutually exclusive.

Further, success with TQM can lead to external recognition, which breeds an additional drain on time and resources. The price for progress is having to respond to many inquiries and requests for help from external organizations. In the face of added demands, it is easy for employees to become burned out.

Necessity of Long-Term Focus. Traditionally, management does not have patience for long-term strategies; quick fixes are preferred. However, experience indicates that successful TQM implementation can take five or more years. Unfortunately, many problems faced in higher education cannot wait five years to be solved. Therefore some question the benefit of TQM because it sometimes cannot effectively address immediate issues and problems.

Additionally, some student affairs leaders may be unwilling to make the personal and professional sacrifices needed to successfully implement TQM. Not only is long-term commitment of personal time and energy required, but long-term commitment of employee time and resources is required as well.

Limited Usefulness in Dysfunctional Units. Many organizations contain one or more dysfunctional units; student affairs is no exception. Examples of behavior in dysfunctional units includes severe backbiting and infighting, employees actively working to undermine management, and autocratic managers. TQM will not work in dysfunctional units. Trust is necessary for TQM to thrive, and management and employees must be open to change. Management and employees must possess basic skills to interact, cooperate, and collaborate—or must be sincerely willing to learn such skills. When trust is absent, TQM exacerbates difficulties rather than eliminating them.

Employee Difficulty with Process Orientation. TQM is often criticized for being too process-oriented. It is easy for organizations pursuing TQM to become overburdened with a quality bureaucracy. Further, many student affairs professionals were drawn to the profession because of its counseling orientation. Some find it difficult to take the process-oriented view of the workplace that TQM demands. Additionally, those employees with Ph.D.s are highly trained in statistical and analytical tools; some may fail to appreciate the power contained in the simplicity and understandability of TQM tools (Teeter and Lozier, 1991).

Limited Documented Success. It has been estimated that only one-fifth to one-third of TQM programs in the United States and Europe have achieved significant, tangible improvements in quality, productivity, competitiveness, or financial returns (Harari, 1993). Because it is easy to find articles touting the potential benefits of TQM but harder to find hard data to support it, one might question why TQM proponents do not "practice what they preach" by making decisions based on fact and data.

Thoughts About Implementing TQM

Empirical evidence supports the conclusion that TQM can produce valuable results in an organization, but it has not done so for all TQM adopters. Also, TQM is not necessary for success (Powell, 1995). Many student affairs operations achieve success, and we assume that they do so without TQM. If, however, after evaluating the pros and cons of TQM a student affairs organization chooses to proceed, steps can be taken to maximize the probability of success (Brigham, 1994c).

Clarity of Mission. It is vital that everyone in the organization understand why TQM is being implemented: to help student affairs fulfill its mission and move toward its vision for the future. Leaders must be able to articulate these reasons clearly and frequently to themselves and others. Implementing TQM will require more effort, be more disruptive, and take longer to achieve results than can be anticipated. TQM is not a quick fix, and therefore everyone in an organization must be willing to invest the time and energy to make it succeed (Lewis, 1994).

Leaders as Models. Leadership cannot be stressed enough. It seems the only organizations to succeed in implementing TQM are the ones whose tireless leaders constantly ask, "What have we done today to improve quality for our customers?" Student affairs leaders must be persistent and not easily discouraged; TQM results take time (Howard, 1994a). Further, student affairs leaders must be visibly involved in implementing TQM practices. Involvement by leaders means demonstrating TQM practices rather than just talking about them. Employees will question whether leaders' personal behavior measures up—whether they "walk the talk." Student affairs leaders must attend TQM training sessions alongside frontline employees. An additional option is to devote part of the agenda of senior staff meetings to discuss TQM issues. This can be as simple as reading and discussing books or articles on TQM.

When leaders become aware of comments about their inability to model quality principles, they have a choice about how to react. If they get angry and defensive, employees will use those emotional reactions to discredit TQM. It is better to focus on TQM as a journey in which everyone in student affairs is learning what the principles and practices of TQM mean. It is important to admit that everyone has much to learn (Holmes, 1994). In fact, the best learning comes from experience. "A leader who attempts to introduce [TQM] without personally experiencing the change will not appear authentic nor trustworthy to his or her organization" (Pickett, 1994).

Culture Change. To successfully implement TQM, culture change must occur. Planning for and supporting cultural transformation is important, as is recognizing that any model of implementation must be tailored to your environment. Develop a comprehensive implementation plan that truly incorporates strategic planning, process reengineering, continuous improvement teams, and individual employee empowerment. Too many organizations have focused on one aspect (for example, TQM teams) and then have been frustrated by their inability to achieve the culture change they seek (Howard, 1994b). "The goal isn't a perfect adoption of the perfect model; it's a system for and commitment to quality that will work for your institution" (Kovel-Jarboe, 1994a).

Invest Time and Energy. Student affairs leaders must accept that it will take a considerable amount of time and even more energy to implement TQM. Leaders must motivate, reward, and counsel those who are attempting this very fundamental change (Kovel-Jarboe, 1994b). It takes significant time to learn and understand quality concepts and values.

Final Words

Student affairs leaders should give thoughtful consideration before implementing TQM. "Near-evangelical, unwavering, long-term commitment" by leaders is critical for TQM's success (Powell, 1995, p. 19). Top managers must be willing to devote personal time and energy to ensure success. Further, leaders must be willing to commit to the long haul—a difficult challenge in modern organizations in which "management plans often have the shelf life of cottage cheese" (Mathews, 1992, p. 48).

Student affairs leaders might be well advised to ask themselves several questions before implementing TQM (Lozier, 1994):

Do you truly understand the principles underlying [TQM]?
Do you truly embrace these principles, or can you at least articulate clearly what principles are being embraced?
Do you have a vision for student affairs, and are the principles that underlie TQM inherent in that vision?
If asked, could you present a session on the principles of TQM?

Is the TQM thrust a genuine interest in continuous improvement, or a ruse that is seen as a counter to public outcries for accountability or decreases in public financial support?
Are you committed to the long-term effort that producing real change requires?
Are you willing to base decisions on fact rather than perception?

For organizations pursuing high performance, the emphasis should be on realistic expectations of improving both operational results and customer satisfaction, not on "doing quality" or some other specific program. Student affairs units can develop creative, adaptive, flexible approaches to achieve high performance in ways that fit their unique cultures and diverse missions. If successful, student affairs professionals might discover that the potential benefits of TQM are innumerable.

References

Brigham, S. "Preface." In AAHE Continuous Quality Improvement Project, *Twenty-Five Snapshots of a Movement: Profiles of Campuses Implementing CQI.* Washington, D.C.: American Association for Higher Education, 1994a.

Brigham, S. (ed.). *CQI-L: Recommendations to Leaders.* [cqi-1@MR.Net]. June 24, 1994b.

Brigham, S. "Questions on Resistance to CQI." In S. Brigham (ed.), *CQI-L: Synthesized Response.* [cqi-1@MR.Net]. Feb. 3, 1994c.

Eskildson, L. "TQM's Role in Corporate Success: Analyzing the Evidence." *National Productivity Review,* Autumn 1995, pp. 25–38.

Greising, D. "Quality: How to Make It Pay." *Business Week,* Aug. 8, 1994, pp. 54–59.

Harari, O. "Ten Reasons Why TQM Doesn't Work." *Management Review,* Jan. 1993, pp. 33–38.

Harris, J. W., and Baggett, J. M. (eds.). *Quality Quest in the Academic Process.* Birmingham, Ala.: Samford University, 1992.

Henthorne, M. "Systems Thinking: Tapping Every Employee's Intellect and Creativity." *Bulletin of the Association of College Unions–International,* May 1993, pp. 30–32.

Holmes, R. "Leaders as Models." In S. Brigham (ed.), *CQI-L: Recommendations to Leaders.* [cqi-1@MR.Net]. June 24, 1994.

Howard, N. "Leaders as Models." In S. Brigham (ed.), *CQI-L: Recommendations to Leaders.* [cqi-1@MR.Net]. June 24, 1994a.

Howard, N. "Models and Plans for Implementation." In S. Brigham (ed.), *CQI-L: Recommendations to Leaders.* [cqi-1@MR-Net]. June 24, 1994b.

Kovel-Jarboe, P. "Models and Plans for Implementation." In S. Brigham (ed.), *CQI-L: Recommendations to Leaders.* [cqi-1@MR.Net]. June 24, 1994a.

Kovel-Jarboe, P. "Time and Energy." In S. Brigham (ed.), *CQI-L: Recommendations to Leaders.* [cqi-1@MR.Net]. June 24, 1994b.

Lewis, R. "Clarity of Mission." In S. Brigham (ed.), *CQI-L: Recommendations to Leaders.* [cqi-1@MR.Net]. June 24, 1994.

Lozier, G. "Questions Leaders Must Ask." In S. Brigham (ed.), *CQI-L: Recommendations to Leaders.* [cqi-1@MR.Net]. June 24, 1994.

Mathews, J. "The Cost of Quality." *Newsweek,* Sept. 7, 1992, pp. 48–49.

National Institute of Standards and Technology. *Malcolm Baldrige National Quality Award: 1995 Education Pilot Criteria.* Gaithersburg, Md.: National Institute of Standards and Technology, 1995.

National Institute of Standards and Technology. *Malcolm Baldrige National Quality Award: 1996 Award Criteria.* Gaithersburg, Md.: National Institute of Standards and Technology, 1996.

Peachy, B. "Types of Resistance in Attempting to Implement CQI." In S. Brigham (ed.), *CQI-L: Synthesized Response.* [cqi-1@MR.Net]. Feb. 3, 1994.

Pickett, W. "Leaders as Models." In S. Brigham (ed.), *CQI-L: Recommendations to Leaders.* [cqi-1@MR.Net]. June 24, 1994.

Powell, T. C. "Total Quality Management as Competitive Advantage: A Review and Empirical Study." *Strategic Management Journal,* 1995, *16,* 15–37.

Roberts, H. V. (ed.). *Academic Initiatives in Total Quality for Higher Education.* Milwaukee, Wis.: ASQC Quality Press, 1995.

Senge, P. *The Fifth Discipline.* New York: Doubleday, 1992.

Seymour, D. *High Performing Colleges.* Vol. 1. Maryville, Mo.: Prescott, 1996.

Seymour, D., and Collett, C. *Total Quality Management in Higher Education: A Critical Assessment.* Methuen, Mass.: GOAL/QPC, 1991.

Teeter, D. "Unique Themes." In S. Brigham (ed.), *CQI-L: Recommendations to Leaders.* [cqi-1@MR.Net]. June 24, 1994.

Teeter, D., and Lozier, G. "Should Institutional Researchers and Planners Adopt TQM?" In L. Sherr and D. Teeter (eds.), *Total Quality Management in Higher Education.* New Directions for Institutional Research, no. 71. San Francisco: Jossey-Bass, 1991.

Walton, M. *The Deming Management Method.* New York: Putnam, 1986.

NANCY LEE HOWARD is director of the office of quality and continuous improvement at Oregon State University.

If total quality management is to become a significant paradigm for student affairs, we must seek a more consistent connection between total quality concepts and the student learning mission.

TQM: Finding a Place in Student Affairs

Tyrone A. Holmes

Much has been written about total quality management (TQM) and its tools and philosophies. Since the late 1980s many books and articles, consultants, and experts have provided glowing accounts of TQM and its promise for higher education (Entin, 1993). Many institutions, following the lead of pioneering colleges and universities, moved to adopt TQM principles and practices to improve administrative practices, teaching methods, student achievement, communication processes, and institutional maintenance (Horine, Hailey, and Rubach, 1993).

Recent evidence demonstrates that the honeymoon for TQM may be over, however. Widespread criticism has been reported by administrators, staff, and students (Entin, 1994; Seymour, 1993). Once seen by some as a panacea for higher education, TQM is now seen by many as just another management fad. This raises the question of whether TQM can play a significant role as institutions attempt to incorporate quality assurance into their educational programs and services.

This chapter takes a critical look at the TQM paradigm. The concepts and practices of TQM are examined, as is their failure to live up to expectations in higher education. Particular attention is paid to the problems inherent with TQM initiatives in an educational environment. Ways in which TQM philosophy and practice can be proactively applied by student affairs to support the academic mission of the university are also discussed.

Barriers to Effective TQM Implementation

Total quality management is an administrative approach geared toward long-range success through customer satisfaction. It is based on the participation of all employees in the continuous improvement of organizational processes, products, services, and culture. The great intuitive appeal of TQM philosophies explains the widespread adoption of TQM initiatives in higher education. Despite this appeal, however, TQM is close to becoming outdated.

Process Focus. A fundamental principle of TQM is an ongoing focus on process improvement. Institutions implementing TQM operate on the premise that every organization is a network of important processes and systems; attention to these processes should therefore be a primary consideration in the management of any organization. Organizational process improvement has unfortunately become a primary goal instead of a means to an end (Myers and Ashkenas, 1993). Educational institutions must seek to improve outcomes— not merely enhance and stabilize the processes that might lead to these outcomes. Such an approach is what McLagan (1991, p. 31) refers to as "process rigor mortis": the tendency of some institutions to attempt to make all work processes routine, but failing to consider the direct impact of these processes on desired organizational outcomes. Similarly, Brigham (1993) disputes the notion that if you focus on the basic processes of an organization, then achieving positive outcomes is inevitable. He emphasizes that although process goals are often met in many TQM initiatives, outcome goals are not always achieved. He recommends that if TQM is to be successful, higher education institutions must find a balance between focusing on processes and results.

Quality Bureaucracies. A second problem found within many existing TQM initiatives is the tendency to create cumbersome quality bureaucracies. Philosophically, TQM is about empowering employees, sharing information, managing work through collaborative teams, and the decentralization of organizational structures and practices. In theory, everyone is responsible for quality improvement and employees are given the authority and responsibility to address relevant issues and problems.

In reality, however, TQM programs have created bureaucratic structures that inhibit true employee empowerment, creativity, and teamwork: quality councils headed by a TQM manager, quality departments, quality lead teams, and quality improvement teams, to name a few (Berry, 1991).

These councils and departments have the primary responsibility for leading the organization down the TQM path. What is created, however, is a structure that removes responsibility from those closest to the work itself. Harari (1993) emphasizes this concern when he states that "TQM delegates quality to quality czars and experts rather than to real people" (p. 34). What results is the further development of a centralized bureaucracy that inhibits the accomplishment of some of TQM's most basic objectives, such as employee participation in decision making and team-based work activities.

Customer Involvement. Another concern regarding current TQM programs involves the failure of institutions to include customers in the quality improvement process. Perhaps this is understandable given the difficulty that colleges and universities have in identifying their internal and external customers and in focusing energy on addressing the needs of these diverse constituencies. Although most educators would agree that students are primary benefactors of educational outcomes, many are opposed to a philosophy that labels students as customers (Winter, 1991).

Nonetheless, the most fundamental TQM concepts include a commitment to quality as defined by the customer. A keen sense of customer needs and wants drives all activities in the TQM organization. If TQM programs are to be successful, higher education institutions must clearly identify all customers—particularly students—and involve them in the quality improvement process. Failure to do so has led many institutions to spend great amounts of energy on activities that are trivial or irrelevant to customer needs (Brigham, 1993).

Leadership Involvement. Accompanying the lack of customer involvement in current TQM initiatives is a lack of top leadership involvement. Organizations implementing TQM are best served by leaders with a strong vision of the future, a willingness to listen to others, and an ability to work as a team member. Such leaders must help provide clear direction and support for the efforts of others.

Many TQM programs lack the strong support required from organizational leadership. In these cases, top management, having only a passive commitment to quality, delegates primary responsibilities to lower management; this creates roadblocks in any large-scale organizational initiative. Without continuing visible participation in TQM efforts from the top, TQM initiatives are likely to suffer (Brigham, 1993).

Higher Education Barriers

Although most problems have plagued both corporate and educational TQM initiatives, colleges and universities have a unique set of barriers with which to contend. Perhaps the greatest barrier is adapting TQM's corporate management philosophy to a higher education context.

Terminology. The first barrier involves the terminology used in the TQM paradigm. TQM has its roots in statistical process control (SPC) and was originally conceptualized as a manufacturing management model. Although its form has changed somewhat from the time when W. Edwards Deming and Joseph M. Juran introduced the concepts to Japan after World War II, it is still replete with engineering and statistical concepts.

Terms such as *cause-and-effect diagrams, kaizen, benchmarking, common-cause variation,* and *plan-do-check-act cycles* continue to be common in TQM language. Except for business and engineering faculty, such terms are foreign to most in higher education, and have interfered with the smooth transition of TQM practices into the academy (Carothers, 1992).

Organizational Culture. A second barrier relates to the unique organizational culture found in higher education institutions. Whereas most corporate entities tend to be hierarchical organizations with clear objectives and a formal chain of command, educational institutions are often more democratic in nature, with overlapping spheres of influence at every level. These "organized anarchies" are not rational and harmonious entities—they consist of shifting coalitions that bargain for desired outcomes, each of which uses various strategies to influence results. Although most colleges and universities have mission statements, these statements do not always reflect shared organizational visions and objectives (Birnbaum, 1991).

The institutional culture of higher education has inhibited the smooth transition of TQM's practices and philosophies. This is particularly true for the teaching and research elements of the institution. In fact, the lack of enthusiasm from faculty is probably the single greatest reason that TQM may become nothing more than a management fad. Clearly, the most prodigious application of TQM initiatives has occurred in the business element of higher education (Brigham, 1993; Marchese, 1991).

Except for business and engineering departments, in which clear connections to TQM philosophy can be found, some faculty have been reluctant to involve themselves in TQM initiatives. One reason for this reticence is the perceived incompatibility between the unique culture of higher education and the TQM paradigm. Another reason is that faculty tend to be individualistic and limit their commitment to their programs and academic units. They are generally less interested in campuswide processes and operations. Such a perspective is antithetical to total quality philosophy which seeks to find congruence and commitment across organizational units (Winter, 1991).

Management Fad. A third barrier to the implementation of TQM in higher education is that TQM is seen as another in the long line of management fads. Faculty believe that the TQM movement is not likely to last and therefore does not need to be taken seriously. A number of institutions initially jumping on the TQM bandwagon have now actually backed off, citing other priorities such as building culturally plural communities and dealing with more immediate crises such as budget deficits. In addition, faculty already believe that they are providing quality education to students and fail to see how a corporate paradigm can help with classroom teaching and scholarly work (Entin, 1994).

Horine, Hailey, and Rubach (1993), however, find that although the greatest concentrations of quality improvement efforts are in administrative areas, an increasing number of colleges and universities are applying TQM initiatives to teaching practices. Likewise, although Brigham (1995) acknowledges that most TQM programs are administrative in nature, he believes that more TQM initiatives are taking place in the academic arena. Such initiatives include addressing concerns with undergraduate curriculum, classroom teaching, and offering classes related to TQM. Many of these practices are still limited to business and engineering departments, however. Unless faculty members across various disciplines embrace TQM concepts and practices, it will always be in danger of becoming obsolete.

In spite of these barriers, TQM concepts have much to offer to student affairs and to higher education in general. Few educators would argue against consistently focusing on quality services, developing and empowering employees, or improving organizational processes. The ineffective applications of these concepts, however, coupled with the inherent difficulties of incorporating a business philosophy in higher education, have led many to question the efficacy of the TQM paradigm. If TQM is to find a place in educational institutions, a model for its implementation must be developed. Such a model must be based on the unique issues and cultural variables found within higher education institutions. With this purpose in mind, the remainder of this chapter will specifically examine how TQM philosophy and practice can be effectively used within student affairs and higher education.

TQM's Place in Student Affairs

If TQM is to become a permanent fixture in higher education, two things must occur. First, the well-documented implementation problems plaguing many TQM initiatives must be addressed. Second, and more important, such initiatives must be consistently geared toward the facilitation of student learning and development. It is here that student affairs can most effectively use TQM principles and processes.

The primacy of student affairs' role in the area of student learning and development has been expressed in various forums, most recently by the American College Personnel Association (1994) in their Student Learning Imperative (SLI). This document holds that "student affairs professionals are educators who share responsibility with faculty, academic administrators, other staff, and students themselves for creating the conditions under which students are likely to expend time and energy in educationally purposeful activities" (p. 2). Such a philosophy asserts that all student affairs activities must be geared toward the facilitation of specific student learning and personal development outcomes.

The SLI identifies five characteristics of a learning-oriented student affairs division, three of which are: confluence of the student affairs and institutional mission statements, with a primary focus on the enhancement of student learning and personal development; resource allocations based on student development objectives; and collaboration between student affairs and other institutional offices in the promotion of student learning and personal development. Additionally, the learning-oriented student affairs division recognizes that professional staff are experts on student life, teaching processes, and learning environments. As such, student affairs professionals consistently examine institutional practices and policies to determine if they facilitate student learning. They also ensure that student affairs policies and practices are based on current student learning research and institution-specific assessment data.

The TQM paradigm has much in common with the philosophy espoused in the SLI. Both are geared toward quality improvement based on customer needs. With the SLI, quality is specifically defined by the extent to which students learn and develop. Both are focused on developing collaborative relationships between key offices and individuals. Both involve a focus on process and encourage the use of data in decision making. In fact, because of this philosophical confluence, student affairs can effectively develop learning-oriented divisions through the purposeful application of TQM principles and practices.

Specifically, student affairs professionals must define quality and customer service, use data in management decision making, continually seek to improve quality, vigorously develop human resources, effectively use quality improvement teams, and provide visionary leadership.

Defining Quality and Customer Service. As previously indicated, defining quality and identifying customers is not a simple matter. Carr (1990) underscores the evasiveness of the quality concept when he provides three definitions: process quality, product quality, and benefit quality. Process quality is the extent to which a particular organizational process reliably produces the desired output. Quality exists when the process generates no scrap or rework and is completed on time. Process quality is best identified with the slogan, "Do it right the first time."

Product quality depends on, but is different from, process quality. Product quality is the extent to which a completed product or service performs as expected when it is delivered. It is best identified with the idea of conformance to requirements. Benefit quality is the extent to which the product or service provides the expected outcomes for the customer; it is the most elusive of the three, and is suggested by the intrinsic and extrinsic value that a customer derives from the product or service. Although all three are important, Carr (1990) emphasizes that benefit quality is an area that organizations often neglect.

Using Carr's (1990) definitions, student affairs professionals can view quality as the facilitation of student learning and personal development. Process quality is exhibited by planning and development procedures that result in efficient, cost-effective programs and services. Product quality is indicated by educational activities that operate as designed, and benefit quality is demonstrated by the measurable enhancement of specific student learning and personal development outcomes. These outcomes include growth in cognitive and intellectual development, psychosocial development, moral and ethical development, and career development.

Pascarella and Terenzini (1991) emphasize the significant impact that out-of-class experiences have on student learning. For instance, the facilitation of students' academic and social involvement, including faculty-student and student-student interactions, can have a positive influence on students' subject-matter learning and critical-thinking skills. Student affairs can and should play a prominent role in the intentional creation of such facilitative programs and environments.

If student affairs is to reach its full potential as a partner with academic affairs in fulfilling the educational role of higher education, and if TQM is to reach its full potential as a management paradigm, a primary area of focus must be the application of TQM principles and practices to student learning and personal development.

Data Use. In order to create programs and environments that facilitate student development, student affairs professionals must rely on the systematic collection and use of information. Because information from many venues is needed, data generated from the instructional systems development (ISD) process is most illustrative. ISD is a systematic process for identifying educational needs, developing programs and services to meet those needs, and then determining if those needs have been met.

Barr and Cuyjet (1991) outline an ISD model that can be effectively applied to student affairs practice. Their six-stage process is designed to facilitate information collection and analysis about the enhancement of student growth. For instance, in the assessment stage, they recommend the collection of information related to current operations, student characteristics and needs, institutional environment, and available human, physical, and financial resources. They further recommend the use of outcomes assessment both to determine the efficacy of programs and services and to use in the administrative decision-making process.

Many parallels have been drawn between outcomes assessment and TQM. Ewell (1991) identified three themes that characterize the emerging best practice in assessment, which are also consistent with total quality philosophy. The first theme is termed *rediscovering process* and involves a focus on information regarding instructional processes, student and teacher behavior, and the connection of courses across the curriculum. The second theme is the use of *naturalistic inquiry* in assessment. Naturalistic inquiry involves using existing points of contact with students as a vehicle for assessment, examining examples of student work, and using current faculty grading processes to yield information useful to instructional improvement. The final theme is the use of *assessment as classroom research*. This emerging movement emphasizes TQM's requirement that employees themselves continuously collect quality-control information.

Similarly, a positive aspect of using the complete ISD process is its confluence with TQM concepts and practices. Macchia (1992) emphasizes this point when he states that the main process outcomes of TQM include improved quality, enhanced organizational effectiveness, and a change in the institutional culture—all of which are primary functions of effectively managed ISD processes.

Systematic data use can be applied by student affairs professionals through the collection of information regarding various student entering characteristics. For example, local data regarding constructs such as career self-efficacy, career decisiveness, and career maturity can be used by career-development specialists to make decisions about appropriate developmental activities. Information regarding exiting characteristics can then be collected to judge the efficacy of educational efforts. Such a process facilitates more effective decision making about program development and resource allocation.

Continuous Quality Improvement. For student affairs to effectively enhance student learning and personal development, continuous efforts must be made to enhance the quality of all programs and services. An integral component of this philosophy is an organizational commitment to the development of student affairs professional staff. Such development must entail training in the various facets and tools of TQM and the application of these tools to student learning and development. Particularly relevant tools include forcefield analysis, benchmarking, focus groups, and the nominal group technique.

Forcefield analysis. Forcefield analysis is a technique that allows a team to examine closely the dynamics of any problem situation. It is based on the notion that any problem, need, or goal is balanced by driving forces and restraining forces. Driving forces are those favoring positive change—accomplishment of a goal; restraining forces are those inhibiting change and goal achievement. By specifically identifying and analyzing each of the driving and restraining forces, student affairs professionals can better understand the underlying issues surrounding a given problem, and thereby develop more effective solutions (Eitington, 1989).

Benchmarking. Benchmarking is a comprehensive study of some specific aspect of a similar high-performance organization. The purpose of this process is to identify a standard against which an organization can measure and improve their way of performing some task or role. For instance, a student affairs department might identify a similar department that performs top-notch new student orientation activities. They can then closely examine how this exemplary department can offer such outstanding programming (Zemke, 1993).

Focus group. A focus group is an interview process in which a relatively small number of individuals (8–12) provide qualitative information in a highly interactive manner. These one-to-three-hour sessions are moderated by a facilitator who selects discussion areas relevant to the educational issue at hand. The ultimate goal of the focus group is to identify opinions, facts, ideas, and solutions geared toward the resolution of problems and the improvement of educational processes (Popham, 1993).

Nominal group technique. Like the focus group, the nominal group technique is used to generate and gather opinions, facts, alternatives, and solutions. Unlike the focus group, however, members represent the group in name only because of the lack of interaction between individuals. This is because of the highly structured information-generating process that allows everyone to participate equally, and prevents any one person from dominating the discussion (Zemke, 1993).

Professional development activities should also include training in ISD concepts and practices. Of particular importance is knowledge of the outcomes assessment process, because TQM initiatives are based on a philosophy of management-by-fact. Student affairs leadership should not assume that student development professionals already possess such knowledge and skills.

Additionally, because TQM principles are not universally accepted in many higher education institutions, programmatic efforts geared toward culture change and organizational transformation must be initiated. This is especially important given the indications that the inadequate management of such change is a barrier to effective TQM implementation (Lozier and Teeter, 1993; Seymour, 1991). Educational efforts must have the goals of increasing the professional staff's knowledge of total quality concepts and practices and showing why such practices should be used in student affairs departments.

Use of Quality Improvement Teams. The primary operational unit in any TQM initiative is the quality improvement team. Student affairs can use these self-directed work groups to address issues related to student learning and personal development. Well-developed work teams enjoy several advantages over traditional solo approaches, including increased productivity, quality, and efficiency. Teamwork may also enhance job satisfaction, employee motivation, and morale (Montebello and Buzzota, 1993). However, many TQM initiatives have floundered because of the inappropriate application of quality improvement teams.

Montebello and Buzzota (1993) offer several suggestions for ensuring maximum productivity from teams. Work teams should be formed by a process that combines smaller tasks to make larger modules of work that have a significant impact on the division, institution, or society as a whole. These work modules should enable the team to handle all aspects of a given project and to connect directly with those who will benefit from the work of the group (students). Such a connection facilitates the receipt of direct feedback regarding group performance and effectiveness.

Members of the team should have a variety of skills, talents, and interests, and each should have a stake in the team's success. Finally, the team should have considerable autonomy. They should have the freedom and authority to plan, organize, schedule, and perform their work tasks.

Student affairs can use a variety of quality improvement teams to facilitate student learning and development. These cross-functional work groups can be charged with divisional responsibilities such as student development, professional staff development, needs assessment, outcomes assessment, systems and technology application, and quality assurance.

Visionary Leadership. Ultimately, if TQM initiatives are to be successful, they must be strongly endorsed by student affairs leadership. Chief student affairs officers must place student learning and personal development at the forefront of the student affairs mission and must work as both partners and supporters of academic affairs in the accomplishment of this goal. Student affairs can also provide leadership to the campus community in the application of TQM principles in a way designed to facilitate such learning and development. Anything short of this goal will risk turning TQM into just another management fad.

Concluding Comments

The principles and practices of TQM can occupy a significant place in student affairs and higher education. Many philosophies espoused by the academy find confluence with the basic tenets of TQM. Actualizing that connection, however, is not a simple task. TQM brings baggage that inhibits its smooth entry into colleges and universities. If it is to become a significant paradigm for student affairs, a more consistent focus on the connection between TQM and the student learning and development mission must be sought.

References

American College Personnel Association. *The Student Learning Imperative: Implications for Student Affairs.* Washington: American College Personnel Association, 1994.

Barr, M. J., and Cuyjet, M. J. "Program Development and Implementation." In T. K. Miller and R. B. Winston, Jr. (eds.), *Administration and Leadership in Student Affairs: Actualizing Student Development in Higher Education.* Muncie, Ind.: Accelerated Development, 1991.

Berry, T. H. *Managing the Total Quality Transformation.* New York: McGraw-Hill, 1991.

Birnbaum, R. *How Colleges Work: The Cybernetics of Academic Organizations and Leadership.* San Francisco: Jossey-Bass, 1991.

Brigham, S. E. "TQM: Lessons We Can Learn from Industry." *Change,* 1993, *25,* 42–48.

Brigham, S. E. "CQI Successes." *American Association of Higher Education Bulletin,* 1995, *47,* 6–9.

Carothers, R. L. "Trippingly on the Tongue: Translating Quality for the Academy." *American Association for Higher Education Bulletin,* 1992, *45,* 6–10.

Carr, C. "Total Quality Training." *Training,* 1990, *27,* 59–65.

Eitington, J. E. *The Winning Trainer.* (2nd ed.) Houston, Tex.: Gulf, 1989.

Entin, D. H. "TQM on Campus: Boston: Less Than Meets the Eye." *Change,* 1993, *25,* 28–31.

Entin, D. H. "Whither TQM?: A Second Look." *American Association for Higher Education Bulletin,* 1994, *46,* 3–7.

Ewell, P. T. "Assessment and TQM: In Search of Convergence." In L. A. Sherr and D. J. Teeter (eds.), *Total Quality Management in Higher Education.* New Directions for Institutional Research, no. 71. San Francisco: Jossey-Bass, 1991.

Harari, O. "Ten Reasons Why TQM Doesn't Work." *Management Review,* 1993, *82,* 33–38.

Horine, J. E., Hailey, W. A., and Rubach, L. "Shaping America's Future: Total Quality Management in Higher Education." *Quality Progress,* 1993, *26,* 41–60.

Lozier, G. G., and Teeter, D. J. "The Challenge: Overcoming the Pitfalls." In D. J. Teeter and G. G. Lozier (eds.), *Pursuit of Quality in Higher Education: Case Studies in Total Quality Management.* New Directions for Institutional Research, no. 78. San Francisco: Jossey-Bass, 1993.

Macchia, P. "Total Quality Education and Instructional Systems Development." *Educational Technology,* 1992, *32,* 17–21.

Marchese, T. "TQM Reaches the Academy." *American Association for Higher Education Bulletin,* 1991, *44,* 3–9

McLagan, P. "The Dark Side of Quality." *Training,* 1991, *28,* 31–33.

Montebello, A. R., and Buzzota, V. R. "Work Teams That Work." *Training and Development,* 1993, *47,* 59–64.

Myers, K., and Ashkenas, R. "Results-Driven Quality . . . Now!" *Management Review,* 1993, *82,* 40–44.

Pascarella, E. T., and Terenzini, P. T. *How College Affects Students: Findings and Insights from Twenty Years of Research.* San Francisco: Jossey-Bass, 1991.

Popham, W. J. *Educational Evaluation.* (3rd ed.) Needham Heights, Mass.: Allyn & Bacon, 1993.

Seymour, D. T. "TQM On Campus: What the Pioneers Are Finding." *American Association for Higher Education Bulletin,* 1991, *44,* 10–13.

Seymour, D. T. *Total Quality Management in Higher Education: Clearing the Hurdles.* Methuen, Mass.: GOAL/QPC, 1993.

Winter, R. S. "Overcoming Barriers to Total Quality Management in Colleges and Universities." In L. A. Sherr and D. J. Teeter (eds.), *Total Quality Management in Higher Education.* New Directions for Institutional Research, no. 71. San Francisco: Jossey-Bass, 1991.

Zemke, R. "A Bluffer's Guide to TQM." *Training,* 1993, *30,* 48–55.

TYRONE A. HOLMES is assistant professor of counselor education at Wayne State University. His research interests include career development, student development, and multicultural counseling and communication.

As the need for accountability increases, student affairs professionals
find it imperative to develop appropriate planning models that
incorporate assessment efforts and resource allocation procedures.

Tying Resource Allocation and TQM into Planning and Assessment Efforts

Richard H. Mullendore, Li-Shing Wang

Student affairs administrators are constantly challenged in their attempts to lead a student affairs division in a productive direction by providing quality services and programs that not only meet student needs but also cultivate student learning and development. A further challenge is to determine how to integrate programs and services into the overall institutional mission and goals while preserving the viability of those programs in the institution's resource allocation process. To meet these challenges, an appropriate planning process must be developed that incorporates quality improvement efforts, assessment measures, and resource allocation procedures. In the current era of budget decline, restructuring, and downsizing, student affairs staff must be aggressive, proactive, and factual in efforts to justify budget maintenance or enhancement.

The University of North Carolina at Wilmington (UNCW) Division of Student Affairs was recently commended by the Southern Association of Colleges and Schools (SACS) reaccreditation team for its assessment efforts. Since 1985, UNCW has been a leader in the implementation of standards issued by the Council for the Advancement of Standards (CAS) for Student Services/Development Programs and the integration of the standards into the planning and annual reporting processes. Now that UNCW has committed itself to TQM, its student affairs division has refined the planning process to adopt TQM concepts. As the assessment movement grows and strengthens, and as many institutions subscribe to the quality movement, it is important that processes and reporting be focused and integrated in a simple, logical manner. Equally important is a planning process tied directly into departmental, divisional, and university budgeting processes. Resource allocation for student affairs programs and departments is now dependent on prior planning and assessment efforts.

Planning models are plentiful; integrated planning processes that connect planning, reporting, TQM, assessment, professional standards, and resource allocation, however, are not as common. The student affairs division at UNCW has developed a comprehensive planning model that incorporates these components. This model has evolved over the past several years and remains flexible because it is refined annually. Use of this planning process has provided the staff with a wonderful tool for developing and enhancing quality services and programs. This chapter describes the evolution of the model and presents the current model in a step-by-step manner for the reader.

Moving from Management by Objectives to Total Quality Management

In 1984, the UNCW Division of Student Affairs planning model was adapted from Deegan and Fritz (1975). It was based on management-by-objectives (MBO) principles and used worksheets for key program results (major components of each functional area), problem-solving objectives (identification of results that do not meet accepted minimal standards), and innovative goals (desired change or new directions for a functional area) (Bryan and Mullendore, 1991). Although the Deegan and Fritz model incorporates both qualitative and quantitative approaches, it served the division well, particularly in its emphasis on quantitative data that assisted each functional area in the development of a database important to its operation. In addition, attention to unacceptable program results led staff to annually address problem areas and recommend changes. Finally, the use of innovative goals became the driving force for positive program and budget changes. The introduction of the MBO model to the student affairs division at UNCW marked a dramatic turn for the division from no planning model to a working planning model that was sharpened and revised as the division grew.

Review of MBO Model. Change has occurred annually in a continuous effort to sharpen the planning process focus and help the division improve the quality of its work. After several years of using the MBO model, top administrators in the UNCW student affairs division evaluated the model, assessed the environment, and felt there was a need for change. As the division continued to improve its planning process, the university (under new leadership) decided to commit itself to TQM principles. Major revisions had to be made to the division's planning model so that concepts and terminology were congruent with the institution's approach. Through the annual planning review the division realized that MBO had served well in the division's growth mode, but the model also contained weaknesses that made continued use of the model somewhat incompatible with TQM. Before discussing the weaknesses of the MBO model, it should be noted that the motivation for change at UNCW was the proactive continued pursuit of excellence rather than a reaction for survival or increasing pressure for accountability.

MBO Weaknesses. Through reexamination of the MBO model, the division became aware that staff found it easier to provide quantitative rather than qualitative measures of success. Although MBO may be helpful in generating necessary quantifiable data, it does not place enough emphasis on accommodating qualitative assessment measures. The emphasis is on achieving objectives, not on assessing objectives or outcomes. For example, an objective of a required orientation program was to project the number of students to be served by the program. In reality, the number of students served was totally dependent on the admission yield (the size of the first-year and transfer classes) in a particular year and was unrelated to the quality of the orientation program. Although it is important to predict how many students will attend orientation (for planning), it is equally important to determine the quality of the program itself through both quantitative and qualitative assessment measures. In another example, an objective of providing programming to residential students was to project the number of programs provided and the number of students who participated. Although both numbers are important, it is essential to address the quality and impact of the programs.

Second, TQM principles are focused on the needs of the customer. Student affairs programs are often provider-driven; MBO provides a comfortable gateway for staff to continue to focus on departmental needs, goals, and objectives rather than customer needs. At UNCW, the shift from MBO to TQM required staff in all functional areas to more adequately assess and respond to student needs (as well as those of other constituencies served). For example, a university union and campus activities staff may seek to provide a year-long series of fifty small, culturally diverse events, even though students desire a smaller number of popular, large, entertainment events. With limited dollars, the campus activity program may need to shift its focus within the TQM framework.

Third, the MBO model tends to reward a functional area for achieving numerical objectives, independent of other functional areas in student affairs. The MBO model allows units to have loose connections, but TQM principles call for "a structured system for creating organizationwide participation in the planning and implementing a continuous improvement process. This process should produce results that exceed the expectations of the customer" (Coate, 1992, p. 2). Acceptance of a customer-driven, teamwork approach can result in a higher quality, seamless approach to a variety of functions. For example, Welcome Week at UNCW was once a campus activities program that began when orientation officially ended. Now, orientation, housing, food services, recreation, and activities (along with academic affairs and others) all contribute time and funding to provide a wonderfully coherent, collaborative program that meets many social and academic integration needs of new students.

Experiencing Transition. Shifting from an MBO approach to TQM principles was not a painless process. TQM first requires commitment and involvement from top-level leadership and management. There is a fine line, however, between the commitment and involvement from the top and the possibility of micromanagement of functional areas, which can create feelings of discomfort, lack of trust, and decreased morale. For student affairs staff, the shift from provider-driven to customer-driven services can be especially painful. The question becomes: Are students customers, products, or both, and how can both be adequately addressed? Staff may comment: "Student affairs has been student-focused already, so what are the differences? We are already doing a quality job; why do you want to implement TQM?" It is a painful process for staff to come to the realization that the transition is not a criticism of their work but a process to change the culture—a culture of how we plan, implement, assess, and feed back to the process, a TQM culture that creates an environment for a more meaningful, integrated planning strategy. It can be a slow process to remove the doubts and discomforts of staff as they attempt to adopt the TQM philosophy, understand the division's TQM model, and use the model in their planning process.

To ease the transition from MBO to TQM for staff, several training sessions were offered to explore the rationale for the changes and guide staff through the implementation of the new model. On a positive note, we found that the implementation of the principles of TQM eliminated some previous resistance to planning in general. We also realized that the dialogue for transition has to continue even after the implementation of the TQM planning model. Changing a culture, particularly the move from provider-driven to customer-driven, requires constant discussion with staff.

Planning Model for the UNCW Division of Student Affairs

The current student affairs planning model has evolved over several years and has been refined almost every year. Attempts are made to keep the planning process as simple and minimally time-consuming as possible for staff who are already stretched beyond normal limits. Of course, the planning process is tied directly to the university mission and goals. When a new chancellor arrived in 1990, he articulated several goals for the university that still exist in their initial form. At the same time, the student affairs division developed a series of goals that complement the university's goals. At an off-campus retreat, division staff were asked to identify appropriate division goals that support the more encompassing statement of university goals. The developed goals were refined by department directors who consolidated and narrowed them to a manageable number. All department planning materials must now be tied to one or more of the university goals. All division program planning must directly relate to university and division goals, and the division planning forms provide space for departments to show this relationship.

Previously, the division planning process was completed at the end of the spring semester; the new planning process, however, is timed to precede the university budgeting process. UNCW's budget process typically occurs during the months of March and April. The division's planning process is currently completed in December, which allows January and February for the directors to discuss and develop priorities before beginning the university budget process. The new division planning process is also timed to provide opportunity for true planning to occur. It is spread over two to three months during the fall semester; this allows staff time to evaluate current programs and services and to complete meaningful planning for the next year. This schedule also permits time for interdepartmental collaboration to occur. Important in using TQM concepts is the collaborative work of departments as planning materials are formulated.

Although the planning process is continuous (see Figure 4.1), for better understanding we will discuss the cycle as it relates to the academic calendar. The division of student affairs planning cycle begins in the fall approximately one year before the time that the results of the planning should occur.

Step 1. Planning materials are provided to the directors no later than mid-October and are due to the vice chancellor for student affairs by December 15. Included in the package are university mission and goals statements and the necessary forms. Everyone in each department should be involved in the process and cross-functional collaboration is strongly encouraged.

Following the distribution of planning materials, a brief training session is held that provides instruction for completing all forms: critical processes (annual goals), goal worksheets (innovation, enhancement, and process problems), and professional and personal growth needs (completed for each staff member). All planning is reported on these three forms, which will be

Figure 4.1. Planning Cycle in Student Affairs

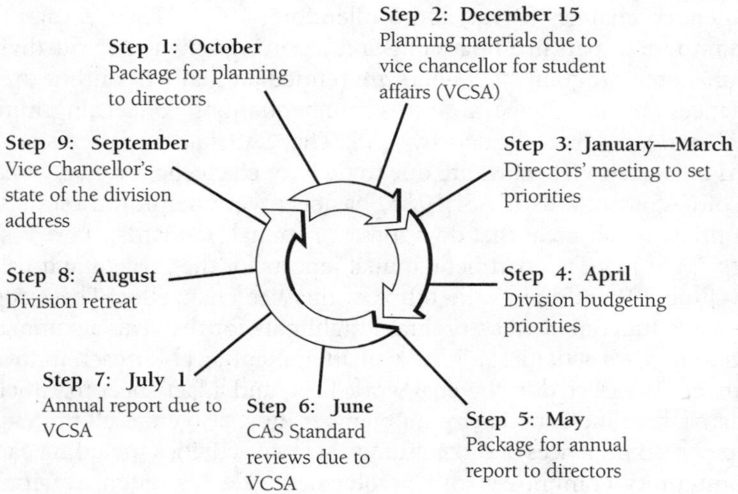

Step 1: October
Package for planning
to directors

Step 2: December 15
Planning materials due to
vice chancellor for student
affairs (VCSA)

Step 9: September
Vice Chancellor's
state of the division
address

Step 3: January—March
Directors' meeting to set
priorities

Step 8: August
Division retreat

Step 4: April
Division budgeting
priorities

Step 7: July 1
Annual report due to
VCSA

Step 6: June
CAS Standard
reviews due to
VCSA

Step 5: May
Package for annual
report to directors

described later. Assessment activities (quality indicators) are tied to each critical process and goal worksheet. Because of the importance that all resource allocation be tied to division and university goals, the forms provide space for this to be done.

Step 2. After receiving the planning materials from directors on December 15, all data are entered into databases. An initial screening is done to compare the current year's data to the previous year's data and to prepare a summary for directors to review.

Step 3. During the period from January to March, division directors meet in a retreat and in their regular meetings to discuss proposed plans for the following year. In these sessions, budgeting needs for each department are presented with rationale for proposed plans (value added) and projected costs. Collaborative efforts in or beyond the division are identified. Tentative division priorities are proposed for funding.

Step 4. About a month later (March to early April), the directors convene again to reach closure on expansion budget priorities. Because of this meeting, consensus ideally is reached regarding student affairs priorities for funding in the coming year. Subsequently this listing is routed through the university budgeting process that asks each division to identify how their priorities aid the university in accomplishing its stated goals.

Step 5. Following the submission of planning materials and the development of budget priorities, the next portion of the planning and reporting cycle occurs during May. At this time, directors receive the package for the annual report, including annual report instructions, the previous year's revision of CAS standards and the department organizational chart, the last three years' fact sheets, and an explanation of codes for staff to enter annual report data.

Step 6. Since 1986, each division functional area has reviewed its program statement (using CAS components) annually to determine current practice and recommended changes (Bryan and Mullendore, 1991). The CAS standards play an important part in all planning and reporting activities in the division. Functional area program statements are refined annually to outline areas of compliance, areas of concern, and recommendations concerning minimal national standards as indicated by CAS. The CAS standards revisions and updated organizational charts are due to the vice chancellor annually on June 1. Use of CAS standards (CAS, 1986) has been very helpful in establishing budget priorities for areas that do not meet national standards.

Step 7. On July 1, department annual reports for the preceding fiscal year (July 1–June 30) are due in the office of the vice chancellor. These reports include each functional area's program highlights for the year, a summary of the previous year's activities, a review of attainment level for each innovation and enhancement listed in the goal worksheet, and a fact sheet that includes quantitative baseline data. Each staff member must also enter all professional development experiences and community service activities including campus and community committees and involvement, classes taught, regional or national conference presentations, leadership positions, publications, professional development activities and workshops, and so on. This information is entered directly into the division's database.

Each director submits a one-page executive summary of the department annual report in order to make the composition of the division's annual report easier for the vice chancellor or associate vice chancellor. Once all departmental annual reports are received, the division's annual report is developed. The division annual report is due to the office of the chancellor by July 15 each year so that it may be forwarded to the system president.

Step 8. Each August, before the opening of school, the division of student affairs convenes a two-day off-campus retreat for professional staff. At that retreat, the tone is set for the coming year as goals and plans are shared. Budget enhancements are usually provided to the division by August 1, contingent on closure of the state legislative session.

Step 9. At the first fall divisionwide staff meeting, the vice chancellor provides for all professional and support staff a verbal summary of the previous year's activities and the goals for the coming year. At this point, the planning process cycle starts over.

Planning Forms: Critical Processes, Goal Worksheet, and Professional and Personal Growth Needs

By mid-October directors receive a package containing information for completing planning materials for the following academic year. The information package includes instructions, university mission and goal summaries, division mission and goal summaries, and three planning forms: critical processes (see Exhibit 4.1), goal worksheet (see Exhibit 4.2), and professional and personal growth needs (see Exhibit 4.3). Training sessions are provided as needed to assist staff in the planning process.

Critical Processes. The development of a program statement (CAS standards) and TQM concepts provide a backdrop for each functional area to identify its critical processes. For each critical process, staff list primary customers; list and group customer needs; name the ongoing processes that fulfill the university, division, and department missions and ensure that customer needs are met; and determine at least one performance measure for each critical process (see Table 4.1). To complete this form, a functional area must link its mission to division and institutional goals and identify their customers and customer needs. An important fact to note is that using this format places assessment activities at the forefront of planning.

For example, the mission of orientation is to provide a program that will assist new students in their transition to the institution; expose them to the educational opportunities; orient them to the academic and cocurricular life of the university; and assist parents in being supportive of their students. This mission supports the university's goal to improve the retention rate of new students and to excel in undergraduate teaching. Critical processes for the orientation program include the processes of selecting orientation leaders, training orientation leaders, annual

Exhibit 4.1. Critical Processes Form

Critical Processes, 1995–96
Annual Cluster Goals

Functional Area: Campus Life Cluster/Housing and Residence Life   Date: December 15, 1994

Program Responsibilities (Critical Processes)	Expected Results (Qualitative Measures)	Assessment Methods (Surveys, Focus Groups, and so on)
"Beginnings:" Welcome Week activities for UNCW campus for Fall 1995	Provide positive campus experience that connects students to each other and to the campus community	Increased attendance for events Fewer discipline cases during the first week Enough opportunities to meet people, higher level of satisfaction and comfort through telephone interviews and focus groups
	Help to establish habits in students that will lead to academic excellence and healthy living	Improved first year retention rates Increased use of student services
	Communicate student development theoretical principles and models to program planning and program participants	Streamline publicity, better communication, collaborative meetings
	Emphasize the benefits of involvement and involvement opportunities to establish a pattern for participation	More students becoming involved on campus; conducting follow-up or referrals made to student organizations

program revision, orientation information distribution, and program delivery (see Table 4.1). Each process has different primary customers and different needs.

Cross-functional collaboration is encouraged in determining critical processes for a functional work area. For example, at the beginning of the fall semester, Welcome Week activities are a critical division process, but several functional areas must work together to make it a successful week. Thus the Campus Life Cluster—including orientation, university union, campus recreation, and student life studies—along with the housing and residence life offices, developed a joint critical process called "Welcome Week activities" in their planning materials. As can be seen, by collaborating, staff can achieve several key elements of TQM: focus on processes, customer-driven emphasis, teamwork and cooperation, mission and customer linkage, and using long-term thinking to see the impact of the program or service on the organization in the future.

Goal Worksheet. Whereas the critical processes form deals with the ongoing services and programs in each functional area, the goal worksheet deals with innovations and enhancements for improving a specific critical process. On the goal worksheet (Exhibit 4.2), departments state the idea (what

Table 4.1. Critical Processes for Orientation

Critical Processes	Primary Customers	Customer Needs	Assessment
Selecting orientation leaders	Enrolled students who meet the requirements	Know when, where, how to apply and what would affect them	Candidate pool
Training orientation leaders	Selected students	Receive adequate training to perform their jobs and feel good about being orientation leaders	Performance during the orientation program
Annual program revision	Orientation advisory group and related departments	Construct a better program with smoother operation	User satisfaction and less on-site trouble shooting
Information distribution	Campus departments and new students	Receive adequate information regarding the program	Fewer phone calls received regarding basic information of orientation program
Program delivery	New students and their parents	Receive adequate information about the university and feel good about attending UNCW	User satisfaction and retention rate from summer orientation to fall semester

Exhibit 4.2. Goal Worksheet Form

Goal Worksheet, 1995–96

❏ Innovation and Enhancement   ❏ Process Problem

Functional Area_____   Division Goal #_____   University Goal #_____

Idea (we wish to)_____

_____

Assumptions/needs_____

Expected results_____

_____

Assessment methods_____

_____

Method of implementing (include request for personnel, space, budget, and so on)   Timetable   Cost

_____   _____   ____

_____   _____   ____

_____   _____   ____

FOR OFFICE USE ONLY: Budget_____   Progress_____ they wish to do); why they think it is needed (and whether it is an innovation or enhancement); the expected results; how would they assess the effort; and how they plan to implement the idea (including a timetable and list of needed resources: staff, time release, money, space, equipment, etc.).

The goal worksheet serves several purposes: first, TQM suggests that 94 percent of a unit's concerns are problems with processes and 6 percent are problems with workers (Deming, 1986). Therefore this planning process emphasizes how to improve and enhance the process rather than how to fix human errors. Staff know how to identify the problems and solutions, and they are willing to improve the processes.

Second, the worksheet deals with continuous change and improvement. Every year staff are asked to offer suggestions for improving the effectiveness and efficiency of programs and services. Again, assessment is a key part of the planning process. For each goal, staff determine how they are going to assess the effectiveness of the program. As mentioned earlier, planning materials are tied to the budgetary process. Through planning materials, staff request the resources they need; this gives the division a starting point for annual budgetary discussions. Significantly, not every innovation or enhancement requires new resources; only those having budget impact, therefore, will be presented in the budgetary discussions.

Third, at the bottom of the goal worksheet, there are two items for office use only: budget and progress. The purpose of these items is to hold accountable both the department and senior student affairs administrators for the plan-

Exhibit 4.3. Professional and Personal Growth Need Form

Professional and Personal Growth Need, 1996–1997	
Name _____ Date _____ I feel I need to grow in:_____ _____ _____ _____ _____ _____ _____ _____	Commitment I intend to make to meet this need: _____ _____ _____ _____ _____ _____ _____ _____
My major concern is: ☐ Knowledge_____ ☐ Skills_____ ☐ Ability_____ ☐ Attitude_____ ☐ Other_____ This deals with growth in: ☐ My profession ☐ My job ☐ Myself as a total person	_____ _____ _____ _____ _____ _____ _____ _____

ning materials. A year after planning materials are submitted, a review of progress is made regarding the accomplishment of each goal and the resulting cost. This review answers two questions: Is progress being made to accomplish goals, and are the necessary resources being allocated to accomplish them? Goal worksheets are used to address TQM concepts of continuous incremental improvement, employee involvement, and the creation of a supportive organizational climate.

Critical Processes and Goal Worksheets. Focusing on critical processes and goal worksheets makes this planning model different from strategic planning. The division addresses strategic planning through retreats for division directors and all staff. The TQM planning model is structured to provide divisionwide participation in the planning and implementation of a continuous improvement process that meets or exceeds the needs of the customers. By tying the planning process to the budgetary process, it is streamlined to eliminate redundancy, top management commitment and involvement in the process is demonstrated, and the planning document becomes a living document rather than more unnecessary paperwork.

On the critical processes and goal worksheet forms, staff are required to determine assessment methods and types of measurement to be used. To be consistent with TQM concepts, all decisions should be based on fact and accurate data. The assessment efforts (including establishment of a routine in collecting basic information, inquiries about user satisfaction and needs, and evaluation of program impact) mandated in the planning process provide the facts and accurate data for further decision making. Also, in student affairs, assessment is often forgotten. Staff know they need resources to deliver their programs and services, but often forget they may need resources to conduct assessment activities as well. Putting assessment measurements on the critical processes form and assessment methods on the goal worksheet is a reminder to staff—assessment is a must and time and resources must be allocated to perform the assessment.

Professional and Personal Growth Needs. The third form is the professional and personal growth needs form (Exhibit 4.3). UNCW's student affairs division has made a tremendous commitment to improve the quality and skills of the workforce. The more knowledgeable and skilled each employee in the organization is, the more effective the organization can be. Staff members (professional and support) can use this form to identify personal and professional growth needs and can negotiate with their supervisors for the support they need, such as release time to pursue other professional activities or money to attend special workshops or training. For example, staff have used this opportunity to take an education leave for a master's program, to attend a month-long residential workshop, or to take some release time to concentrate on their professional writing. This commitment from the top of the division shows staff that division leaders care about staff development and about their professional and personal well-being.

Conclusion

The University of North Carolina at Wilmington has developed a divisional planning model that integrates CAS standards, TQM, annual reporting, assessment, and the resource allocation process. UNCW has been a national leader in the integration of CAS standards into the division's planning and reporting processes. More recently, as the university has committed itself to TQM, the division has refined its planning process to accommodate TQM concepts. This chapter has shown how this integration process has occurred and has outlined key dimensions to the planning process such as critical processes, goal worksheets, and professional and personal growth needs.

The model is changing. It adapts to the times and is always seen as a draft. Implementation of the model requires annual staff training that provides another opportunity to emphasize the value of the planning process.

References

Bryan, W. A., and Mullendore, R. H. "Operationalizing CAS Standards for Program Evaluation and Planning." In W. A. Bryan, R. B. Winston, Jr., and T. K. Miller (eds.), *Using Professional Standards in Student Affairs*. New Directions for Student Services, no. 53. San Francisco: Jossey-Bass, 1991.

Coate, L. E. *Total Quality Management at Oregon State University*. Washington, D.C.: National Association of College and University Business Officers, 1992.

Council for the Advancement of Standards for Student Services/Development Programs. *CAS Standards and Guidelines for Student Services/Development Programs*. Washington, D.C.: Council for the Advancement of Standards, 1986.

Deegan, A. X., and Fritz, R. J. *MBO Goes to College*. Boulder: University of Colorado, 1975.

Deming, W. E. *Out of the Crisis*. Cambridge, Mass.: MIT Center for Advanced Engineering Study, 1986.

RICHARD H. MULLENDORE *is vice chancellor for student life and professor of educational leadership at the University of Mississippi. He was instrumental in developing the integrated planning model now in place at the University of North Carolina at Wilmington, where he served as associate vice chancellor for student affairs.*

LI-SHING WANG *is director of student life studies at the University of North Carolina at Wilmington.*

Implementation of TQM requires both planned staff training and organizationwide culture change. Introducing this change through a comprehensive program review, multiyear evaluation, and planning process involving all staff in a student affairs department is beneficial.

Comprehensive Program Review: Applying TQM Principles

D. David Ostroth

Whether it is known as total quality management (TQM), continuous quality improvement (CQI), business process redesign, or by another name, TQM promises to improve student affairs practice. Staff usually resist new management systems, especially when those systems add work to an already busy schedule and have that administrative ring to them (Van Allen, 1994; Seymour and Collett, 1991). Like other comprehensive management approaches, TQM takes time and effort, so leaders must carefully plan ways of introducing TQM concepts to their staffs.

This chapter reviews one system successfully used to implement TQM principles and techniques in a student affairs department; it also discusses TQM applications in one student affairs department at a large public university. A number of TQM principles are highly compatible with the culture of student affairs work. Foremost is the humanistic thrust of TQM, which assumes that processes, not people, are the focus of problem-solving analysis, and that people within the organization must be empowered to solve process difficulties (Sherr and Lozier, 1991; Marchese, 1991). The TQM system emphasizes the development of human resources—an idea very close to the heart of student affairs. Teamwork and a democratic management style are absolutely consistent with classic student development approaches (Crookston, 1972).

TQM focuses on the customer. Though we may resist seeing students as customers, the emphasis on our clientele as the starting point for improvement is deeply rooted in student affairs literature (American Council on Education (ACE), 1949). TQM also emphasizes the use of data gained through systematic inquiry to guide decisions—another idea compatible with student development philosophy and practice. Both the student development movement and the Student Learning Imperative (SLI) point to continuous learning, growth, and change not only for our students, but for professionals and the organizations in which we work (American College Personnel Association, 1975, 1994; Miller and Prince, 1976).

Despite the natural congruence between TQM principles and our own professional values, natural staff skepticism and inertia must be overcome if effective implementation is to occur. Stretched to the breaking point by budget cutting and downsizing and challenged by the urgency of student problems, student affairs staff are naturally reluctant to make long-term commitments to a system of quality beliefs that seem too new at first. TQM's manufacturing roots also make this system appear too mechanized to some at first. Though many TQM concepts are familiar, many new techniques and tools must be learned and applied. TQM implies change in the whole organization's approach, so that small improvements over time lead to improved quality. There may be occasional dramatic and visible "breakthroughs" (Coate, 1990), but it is the long-term approach to continuous improvement that fashions real change. Hence the commitment to TQM must ultimately be made and kept by everyone in the organization in order to achieve maximum results. Though TQM results have not yet been well measured in higher education, many benefits have been identified (Seymour and Collett, 1991; Seymour, 1994).

If student affairs leaders want to implement TQM, they must carefully plan effective ways of introducing new TQM methodologies and obtain commitment from staff. The approach and packaging of these ideas can be important because educators are naturally cynical toward management systems, especially those filled with acronyms and other jargon.

Comprehensive Program Review as a Focus Mechanism for TQM

Ludeman and Fisher (1989) define and describe a comprehensive program review (CPR) procedure for student affairs units. Their thesis is that a long-term, intensive process of departmental program review—a more structured and participative process than typical accountability strategies—can lead to improved programs and services. They cite other benefits to this strategy, including better communication, improvements in working relationships, and enhanced teamwork. Inherent in this process are emphases on defining a mission and goals ("what we do"); defining the customers of student affairs units and programs ("who we serve"); measuring our activities, impacts, and customer satisfaction (measurement of outcomes); and involving staff at all levels (involvement, empowerment, and teamwork). All these themes are consistent with the TQM model.

Cross (personal communication, 1992) adapted the Ludeman and Fisher model (1989, pp. 252–254) to establish a CPR plan for the Virginia Polytechnic

Institute and State University's department of student affairs. The model includes the following steps:

1. *Preparation.* A preliminary planning phase in which the department head, working with the divisional planning and review committee, plans the issues to be addressed and identifies the staffing structure, the approach, and a timetable for the CPR.

2. *Departmental self-study.* A detailed review within the department that includes examination of missions and goals; relation of department goals to those of the university and the division; identification of customers; assessment of customer satisfaction; resource allocation; quantitative and qualitative outcomes of unit programs and organizational structure; and development of action plans to improve processes, services, and programs.

3. *College or university review.* A detailed review of the department and its self-study by a committee within the institution representing students, faculty, and staff with membership from all populations served by the department.

4. *External review.* A campus visit, review, and report by one or more consultants with special expertise in the department's area.

5. *Strategic planning.* Development of a long-range strategic plan by the department, after consideration of the results developed in all preceding phases. The strategic plan includes planning for the methodology by which outcomes are to be measured.

Approximate timetables for these five phases of the CPR were suggested by Cross (personal communicaton, 1992), though each department head was given latitude to define the procedures and time frames most useful for the particular area. The vice president for student affairs mandated that all departments perform comprehensive program reviews under supervision of a division committee chaired by the associate vice president. A staggered schedule was established for CPR cycles.

CPR Implementation in the Department of University Unions and Student Activities

The university unions and student activities department (UUSA) began its CPR cycle in summer 1993. Before beginning the CPR, the department's management team planned a structure for the CPR and made several decisions about the process:

All staff, including all career specialties and all levels, were to be actively involved.

TQM principles were to be taught at the beginning of the process and followed throughout the self-study phase so that the CPR would be explicitly used as the vehicle for integrating TQM strategies and philosophy into all departmental functions.

Full staff participation and consensus seeking were primary goals of the process.

The entire CPR plan would emphasize consideration of both "what we do" (stated mission and goals) and "how well we do it" (measurement of efficiency and effectiveness).

Mission assessment was to be the first priority for completion, since the work of other staff teams would be affected by the new mission statement.

The goals of the process were to be critical analysis, practical conclusions, and real change, not the production of lengthy reports.

Preparation Phase (Summer 1993). Before beginning the self-study, the department director obtained assistance from a business process analyst from the university's department of administrative information systems. The consultant, an expert in TQM, planned and conducted two half-day training sessions for all department staff and one additional half-day session for management staff and for individuals with assigned leadership roles in the CPR-TQM process. The content of these sessions was heavily oriented to the TQM model, though very little management jargon was used. Staff were scheduled for training in small groups of seven to ten people. Content included new definitions of teamwork and team roles and strategies, paradigm shifts that can lead to quality, team listening and constructive feedback skills, team problem solving, and process analysis and improvement skills from the TQM literature. Part of the training approach sought consensus about problems in the department that could be addressed through process analysis. Then small teams completed process analysis procedures to develop solutions. This training introduced all staff to the democratic approaches used in TQM process improvement and set the stage for a new approach involving everyone in continuous improvement.

Self-Study (Fall 1993–Mid-Fall 1994). In the CPR self-study process, staff were divided into five teams: a mission assessment team, a customer needs and institutional expectations team, a programs and services team, an administrative issues team, and a coordinating team with members from all other teams to direct team efforts. These teams critically evaluated many aspects of departmental functioning and quality of output. The process resulted in a fifty-three-page written report with a series of appendixes detailing data-gathering activities.

Mission assessment team. The mission assessment team reviewed the university's and student affairs department's mission statements, the university plan, the Council for the Advancement of Standards' (CAS) criteria for functional work areas concerning UUSA responsibility, and other student affairs literature. Extensive discussion of the department's various roles and the central purposes behind these roles was synthesized with the other literature to produce a draft mission statement; this statement was then sent to the other CPR teams for review. Suggestions were returned to the mission assessment team, which incorporated them into a final mission statement. The department director then provided copies of the new mission statement to all department staff and to the vice president for student affairs.

Customer needs and institutional expectations team. This team defined the customers of UUSA. They gathered available information documenting the satisfaction of UUSA customers with department services and assembled measurements of services, including some never before available. At the request of the department's director, a series of customer satisfaction surveys were begun in 1992 and 1993. These surveys were administered periodically to collect data on the reaction of students, faculty, staff, and community members to the services, programs, and events provided in campus unions. The CPR team reviewed the five satisfaction surveys previously completed by graduate student employees, summarized the results, and provided the original reports as appendixes to the self-study report. Studies had been done to measure satisfaction of event sponsors with union services, facilities, and program support; to evaluate reactions to specific services available in the auxiliary student union; to measure customer reactions to food services; and to assess satisfaction with the main union's recreation area and the university chapel.

The team also developed a series of data tables identifying the scope of provided services, which included such things as numbers of reservations by student and nonstudent groups, number of programs and attendees produced by the Union Program Board and at the Memorial Chapel, total customers served in the union recreation areas, customers served in union food services, and the scope of business services such as ATMs, banking transactions in the main union, and tickets sold by the UUSA ticket office. All of the measurement activity by this team not only extended and systematized data already being collected to measure the level of activity by the department, but also pointed up the lack of outcomes measurement. A major challenge for the UUSA staff (and of all student affairs departments) will be to devise new and better ways of measuring and documenting the impact of their work on students and on the institutions they serve. This CPR cycle resulted in the creation of many new data-collection activities that will enable the department to better document its efforts and trends in the future.

Programs and services team. This team first identified the many programs produced by UUSA and then decided to follow the strategy of thoroughly reviewing a select five program areas: staff development, student organization management and leadership training, program production (technical) support, The Perspective Art Gallery, and Venture Out (a series of outdoor recreational programs). For each of these program areas a subcommittee (usually two people) reviewed the program in detail, interviewed the program's staff and customers, and prepared a report. These reports offered important insights into possible improvements for the individual programs, but left the programs and services team believing that it had only scratched the surface: Their original program list included fifty-one services and ten programs that might have been evaluated, so many programs were left unaddressed in this CPR cycle.

Administrative issues team. The administrative issues team discussed many issues within UUSA, including organizational structure and reporting lines; public communication and marketing of the department; internal department communications; budget development practices; decision-making styles and the involvement of all staff in decisions; personnel management, leave, and overtime policies; employee relations; and staff wellness. A number of these areas, of course, were controversial and resulted in spirited discussion and some disagreement. After a period of group processing, however, the team provided analyses and recommendations for change in each area.

Coordinating team. A coordinating team with representation from all teams answered questions affecting more than one team and oversaw the writing of report sections. Completion of an overall UUSA self-study report presented challenges because a variety of individuals completed different sections. Because staff participation was a hallmark of the self-study, the director did not want to place many restrictions on style or content. As a result, first drafts did not fit together into a cogent whole and some reformatting was needed. In retrospect a better plan would have been to specify more structure from the beginning in order to eliminate some later resentment about extra rewriting and some perceptions that management was trying to control the content of reports.

A final section was developed by the director, which excerpted all recommendations made by the teams and listed actions already taken or contemplated. This strategy proved helpful and necessary to assure staff that their recommendations were being considered and either implemented, modified, or rejected for very good reasons. In practice this recommendation section became a long-term agenda because so many new ideas needed evaluation, funding, and implementation over time.

The self-study was by far the most ambitious and time-consuming part of the total CPR process in this unit. Detailed self-studies take enormous time and effort, but if done well they can yield both constructive quality improvement and impressive gains in teamwork and morale.

University Review (Spring 1995). To provide views of UUSA quality from within the institution but outside the department itself, a university review team (URT) was formed in Spring 1995. Chaired by a senior teaching faculty member, the URT included three students (one international graduate student and two undergraduates), two student affairs professionals from other departments, one teaching faculty member, and the business process analyst who had presented TQM training to the UUSA staff. The director and associate director met with the URT at the outset and discussed the self-study report, which was distributed to the URT members. General suggestions were made for the team's work, including a request for a critique of the self-study report. The team was asked for independent analysis of the issues that they felt were most important to the future of UUSA and its customers. When asked, the director of UUSA provided the URT a list of issues he felt were of concern.

The URT met over the course of two months, reviewed the UUSA self-study report, interviewed many department staff both individually and in focus groups, researched several issues that came up in their interviews, and made a seven-page report to the department. This report was shared with all department members and served as a starting point for departmentwide discussions.

External Review (Fall 1995). In October 1995 the department leadership engaged two well-known experts in the field of university unions and student activities to visit the campus and make an overall review of department quality. The consultants were not asked to make detailed reviews of previous reports but were given general department information in preparation for their visit. The consultants' charge was to comment on any aspect of quality and process with emphasis on the following: student response to UUSA services and programs, organizational structure and staffing, quality of facilities, sources of staff satisfaction or dissatisfaction that could be improved, and the scope and appropriateness of departmental services and programs for the campus.

The consultants visited the Virginia Tech campus for two days and ultimately submitted a twenty-three-page review of the UUSA department that included comments on areas of special quality and suggestions for immediate quality improvement and longer-term strategic priorities.

Strategic Planning. At this writing, UUSA is assimilating the results of all studies and preparing a five-year strategic plan. Most of the short-term recommendations for quality improvements have been evaluated, and a majority have been implemented. The strategic planning phase will take at least a semester to complete, with involvement from all staff in the department.

It should be noted that the strategic planning phase was delayed because of a restructuring that brought two new units under the auspices of the director of the UUSA department: the department of recreational sports (which manages intramural sports, advises extramural sports teams, provides fitness programming, and manages recreational facilities on campus) and the Cranwell International Center (which provides immigration services, orientation, student and family programs, and student activities support to international students). Because CPR and TQM activities were well under way before the addition of these two units, they must be oriented to TQM principles and to the work already completed. Our intent is to include them in the strategic planning phase and then incorporate all areas in the next CPR cycle.

Recommendations for Each Phase of Comprehensive Program Review

Based on the UUSA experience at Virginia Tech, the following recommendations are offered to guide each phase of the CPR process.

Preparation Phase
- This is perhaps the most important stage because the structure and expectations of the whole process should be defined here. In this phase, departmental leadership must identify the guidelines, procedures, and expectations that will guide the various teams in their work. Structure not specified here will be more difficult to add later.
- The department director should carefully define the roles of teams being established for the self-study phase. This may take some discussion between

department management staff, and should probably be discussed with the staff as a whole once a general outline has been drafted.

Self-Study Phase
- Expectations should be set for self-study teams regarding measurements to be made. One of the central tenets of TQM is that systematic data collection be used to guide decisions and change. Moreover, in most student affairs units, increased data collection (particularly outcome measures) is needed to support competition for resources within the academy. CPR is a good vehicle for implementing a commitment to improving the design and collection of data to measure department activity, customer satisfaction, and client outcomes.
- A strong coordinating team should be established, with membership from each of the other departmental teams, to discuss and resolve process issues that arise during the self-study. This group should be empowered to make many of the decisions that structure and guide the process but should acknowledge the department director's expectations if they are strong in some areas.
- In the beginning, the department director or the coordinating team should establish an outline and guidelines concerning report preparation. If guidelines are not provided, first drafts will require extensive work before they can be combined. Moreover, staff who prepare drafts may resent changes after their initial writing assignments are completed.
- Summarize all recommendations in a separate section of the self-study report, and write periodic updates giving responses to the recommendations. Staff deserve to know which of their recommendations are implemented. Because some recommendations cannot be implemented, staff should be provided with a rationale for why some recommendations are rejected. Trust in management will suffer if this step is omitted.

University Review Phase
- Include representatives from all major departmental customers on the URT. Be sure students are represented.
- Consider asking a faculty member to serve as chair. Faculty often have valuable insights into student service needs, and the process offers a chance for collegial problem solving and the development of faculty-student affairs partnerships.
- Make support available to the review team at their request, but offer them a high degree of independence in evaluating your operation.
- Be prepared to provide additional information to the review team on request, and support any independent data gathering the team may want to do, including interviews of department staff.

External Review Phase
- Select consultants with special expertise in the areas needing review. Explain the CPR process to them and give them an understanding of the TQM

theme in the overall review. Be sure the consultants are thoroughly familiar with TQM.
- Consultant services can be quite expensive. Consider inviting consultancies
  from colleagues who can be trusted to think independently, yet who offer
  their services at minimal cost. One way to do this is to trade consulting services from colleagues with experience at institutions similar to your own.
- Rather than expecting consultants to read large amounts of material from
  previous phases, give consultants basic information and ask them to comment on quality issues as they see them. This will give a different view than
  the self-study and college and university review reports can offer.
- Contract for a finished consulting report suitable to provide to your vice
  president and to officials external to your division.

Strategic Planning Phase
- Use the recommendations from the self-study, the college and university
  review, and the external review as starting points for developing long-range
  goals.
- Include all staff in the planning process, and make CQI the explicit goal of
  the long-range plan.

Critique of Comprehensive Program Review as a Vehicle for Introducing TQM

CPR was an excellent strategy for introducing TQM philosophy and techniques
to the UUSA staff. Comprehensive program review, as defined by Ludeman and
Fisher (1989) and as adapted by Cross (personal communication, 1992) is an
ambitious process requiring extensive planning and effort. Though staff have
some natural resistance to any addition to their workload, program review is
a reasonable extension of normal annual report activities in a time of increasing accountability demands. CPR offers a structure for implementing TQM
training and ongoing CQI activity without creating the impression that yet
another new management fad is being foisted on overworked staff.

The CPR-TQM approach had many strengths in the Virginia Tech experience. It offered a natural vehicle for staff TQM training and for team building
in a context of quality improvement; simultaneously it engaged all staff in
problem solving and decision making. This approach led staff to generate many
new ideas for both small and large improvements. It empowered staff at all levels to see themselves as empowered to continue suggesting and making improvements to ongoing departmental processes. This vehicle provided impetus
for staff to start many new measurement projects that focused the department
on better long-range planning.

The approach also presented a number of weaknesses and problems. First
among these is the large time investment required, both in the sense of intensity (proportion of total staff time spent) and duration (years spent on the project). Maintaining intensity and focus over long periods, combined with the

time lag between recommendations and implementation, offer real challenges for departmental leadership.

These issues are further complicated if the department is a large and complex one. Definition of a program involves more complex questions than may at first be evident. The comprehensive nature of CPR makes the task more difficult if many different professional specialties come into play, as is true in some larger student affairs departments. Though it may seem natural to orient CPR activities around an entire unit reporting to a major director, some units may be large and diverse enough to make CPR cumbersome. Each unit head must therefore make strategic decisions about how to aggregate organizational areas when planning CPR-TQM cycles. Though detailed analysis may be best done in smaller, more homogeneous units, it is essential that the functions reporting to a major department chair or unit head be considered as a whole when making quality improvements.

A significant logistical challenge is the difficulty of managing frequent meeting schedules over long periods and the need for large meetings to bring together the results of work by smaller teams. The entire CPR-TQM process requires very active communication, large time commitments for meetings, and constant follow-up. This translates into real dollar costs—an investment in quality.

One of the most challenging aspects of this strategy is that giving a voice to all staff stirs up criticism that may not have easy solutions. Staff who receive encouragement to participate in new ways tend to expect that all their ideas will be used, and also assume that management is required to implement their ideas. This point needs to be discussed candidly, in advance, to be sure that all staff enter the process with realistic views on implementation. At the same time, managers entering this new paradigm must consider their own willingness to move toward a more authentic democratic style.

Recommendations for Designing Comprehensive Program Review/TQM Programs

Based on the Virginia Tech experience with this strategy, the following recommendations should be considered in implementing similar programs:

Expect visible, active support for CPR-TQM from departmental leaders. Departments entering into this approach are making major commitments of time and effort for everyone, and leaders must be actively engaged, contributing, committed, and willing to change as the process unfolds. With TQM this commitment is permanent.

Make a commitment to training for all staff. Although nearly all student affairs staff have heard of TQM, considerable training is needed if everyone in the organization is to understand the full meaning of CQI and the change strategies this implies. The commitment to staff development in this area must be ongoing for maximum effectiveness.

Involve everyone in the organization. A basic tenet of TQM is that persons closest to processes are best able to understand how improvements can be made (Seymour and Collett, 1991).

Introduce group process training and team building. Though professionally trained student affairs staff may be quite familiar with group process, efficient team functioning will require familiarizing all staff with concepts of team roles and effective team member behaviors.

Set clear expectations for process and outcomes. If TQM means new paradigms, the leadership must define specific expectations for this change clearly. If this step is not taken, one can expect role confusion and impasse.

Make sure staff members understand their role in recommending changes, and that administrators understand their accountability to staff for recommendations not implemented. If staff are not used to being invited to provide input and recommendations for change, they may expect administrators to implement all changes they suggest. The difference between input and decision-making authority must be made clear. At the same time, administrators inviting this input must accept accountability to their staffs for explaining why some recommendations could not be implemented. If this critical step is omitted, the integrity of the process becomes suspect and staff commitment will suffer.

Use terminology meaningful to the staff. Student affairs is not fond of management-systems jargon (note, for example, the negative reaction one usually hears when mentioning MBO). The important concern is not the use of technical terms but the emphasis on a few essential values: process analysis, participation, commitment to CQI, and measurement. These concepts should be explained in ways that make immediate and intuitive sense to staff.

Write brief and concise reports. TQM implies some major process redesigns, but mainly its results consist of small, continuous, practical changes that improve processes. Long reports are counterproductive because in a business emphasizing human contact and heavy workloads, we do not have time either to write, read, or act on detailed, lengthy reports.

Create new measures of activity levels, customer satisfaction, quality, and outcomes. Student affairs work offers special challenges to measurement. We must find new ways to measure the volume of work we do and we must systematically sample the opinions of our customers of how well we do it. Above all, we must devise new ways of measuring the impact of our work on students and on our institutions.

Look for one or more processes that can be substantially reengineered for breakthrough outcomes. During program reviews there is often some complex process that is considered by staff or customers to be less than satisfactory. If special analysis and redesign efforts are brought to bear on one such process early in the CPR cycle, a dramatic improvement will often be seen. This will in turn motivate staff because they can see the value of the TQM process analysis technique.

Emphasize the value of constant, small quality improvements. Though there could be occasional breakthroughs, substantial change over time is achieved with incremental change.

Reward creativity, participation, and commitment to quality. One critical role of leaders in organizations espousing TQM is to recognize and reward those who demonstrate ongoing commitment to constructive change and who suggest improvements. Contributions to the CPR-TQM process should receive attention and reinforcement from unit leadership in ways that are visible to all staff.

Conclusion

TQM offers major promise in improving student affairs programs and services. Because of the business and manufacturing connotations of this management system and because it represents a major, long-term commitment of effort, student affairs staff can be expected to resist introduction of this approach. This chapter describes the success experienced by one student affairs department in implementing TQM using CPR as a vehicle. Though CPR is also time-consuming, it is a natural outgrowth of ongoing accountability procedures in most departments. The Virginia Tech experience suggests that CPR offers a practical strategy for integrating TQM techniques into the mainstream of departmental self-study and ongoing program evaluation. The power of the TQM approach lies in the participation of all student affairs staff in reviewing processes and in changing the way we do business. TQM is worth our attention because it builds on many of the central values of our profession: continuous growth, human development, emphasis on customers, measurement of accomplishments, and valuing the contributions of each staff member in the education of our students.

References

American College Personnel Association. "A Student Development Model for Student Affairs in Tomorrow's Higher Education." *Journal of College Student Personnel,* 1975, *16* (4), 334–341.

American College Personnel Association. *The Student Learning Imperative: Implications for Student Affairs.* Washington, D.C.: American College Personnel Association, 1994.

American Council on Education. "The Student Personnel Point of View." *American Council on Education Studies,* series 6, no. 13. Washington, D.C.: American Council on Education, 1949.

Coate, L. E. *Implementing Total Quality Management in a University Setting.* Corvallis: Oregon State University, 1990.

Crookston, B. B. "An Organizational Model for Student Development." *NASPA Journal,* 1972, *10,* 3–13.

Ludeman, R. B., and Fisher, R. "Breathe Life into Student Life Departments with CPR: Comprehensive Program Review." *NASPA Journal,* 1989, *26,* 248–255.

Marchese, T. "TQM Reaches the Academy." *AAHE Bulletin,* Nov. 1991, pp. 3–9.

Miller, T. K., and Prince, J. S. *The Future of Student Affairs: A Guide to Student Development for Tomorrow's Higher Education.* San Francisco: Jossey-Bass, 1976.

Seymour, D. "The Return on Quality Investment." In D. Seymour (ed.), *Total Quality Management on Campus: Is It Worth Doing?* New Directions for Higher Education, no. 86. San Francisco: Jossey-Bass, 1994.

Seymour, D., and Collett, C. *Total Quality Management in Higher Education: A Critical Assessment.* Methuen, Mass.: GOAL/QPC, 1991.

Sherr, L. A., and Lozier, G. G. "Total Quality Management in Higher Education." In L. A. Sherr and D. J. Teeter (eds.), *Total Quality Management in Higher Education.* New Directions for Institutional Research, no. 71. San Francisco: Jossey-Bass, 1991.

Van Allen, G. H. "Organizational Performance and Rigidity Can Act as Impediments to TQM." *Journal of College Student Development,* 1994, *35,* 152–153.

D. DAVID OSTROTH is assistant vice president for student affairs and associate professor in the College of Human Resources and Education at Virginia Tech. He is currently director of the professional issues council and a member of the executive council of the American College Personnel Association.

*Through assessment, educators gain valuable information that will
enable them both to answer questions asked by leaders outside higher
education and to determine from within whether their educational
efforts are making a difference.*

Using Assessment to Achieve Quality in Student Affairs

Richard M. Scott

There is increasing public outcry for more accountability and quality in higher education institutions. This plea comes from parents paying higher tuition bills, legislative leaders facing greater public demand for services and programs, and students choosing their postsecondary institutions. Business and industry leaders, not wanting to spend millions in retraining college graduates, expect their new employees to think for themselves and to be good problem solvers. Upcraft and Schuh (1996) believe that the public impression is that colleges and universities are not producing intelligent, competent, and capable graduates.

Assessment can be used to determine how quality is achieved in higher education. This chapter explores the idea of quality, what it means to educators (student affairs professionals in particular), and the role assessment plays in measuring quality. How assessment is used within TQM to measure quality from a customer or stakeholder perspective is examined and compared to traditional uses of assessment. Assessment's place in the TQM movement is also discussed.

What Is a Quality Education?

Since the 1980s, increasing numbers of people in the public sector have begun to believe that colleges and universities have defined the goals of a quality education for themselves for too long. Government and other public officials have also questioned the value and cost of a college education (Erwin, 1991); in 1986, The National Governors' Association called for the identification of measures of educational effectiveness (see Alexander, Clinton, and Kean, 1986). A report by the Southern Regional Education Board (1985) warned that "the quality and meaning of undergraduate education [have] fallen to a point at which mere access has lost much of its value" (p. 231). At least forty states have established some form of mandatory assessment directed at questions of quality in higher education (Marchese, 1990). The basic question being posed from outside education is, What is the value of a college education?

Upcraft and Schuh (1996) list four factors in the current environment that contribute to the public's questioning of higher education's quality and accountability: First, there are too many college graduates who cannot effectively read, write, compute, or think; second, the rising cost of education has led many to question the price versus value received for a college education; third, the quality of instruction at many institutions has declined with larger classes, less faculty who actually teach, and poor academic advising; and fourth, although higher education has become more inclusive and diverse, many within underrepresented groups have lower graduation rates.

In essence, higher education officials are on the defensive and are being asked to prove that they are accountable and that higher education is worthy of public trust. To this end, educational leaders have turned to the assessment of student outcomes as evidence that institutions are progressing on the right path. Colleges and universities want to show higher graduation rates, a well-trained workforce, and more important, evidence of student learning and development from the college experience (Erwin, 1991). Assessment's two major goals are improvement and accountability. Through assessment, educators can answer the questions asked by leaders outside higher education and at the same time determine from within whether their educational efforts are making a difference.

What does the public's questioning of the value of higher education and higher education's search for quality mean for student affairs? Now more than ever, student affairs professionals are being asked to demonstrate that the programs and services they provide make a difference in students' lives (Hanson, 1991), contribute to the success of the institution, and make a positive contribution to the achievement of student outcomes expected by the institution.

In order to affect important student outcomes, student affairs professionals must focus on how and why students learn. They must be able to demonstrate how programs in housing and residence life, counseling, career services, student activities, and so on contribute positively to student outcomes.

Student affairs personnel play a dual role in an institution's success: They offer essential services (housing, health, counseling, and so on) and contribute to the learning and development of individual students. The primary purpose of student affairs according to Upcraft and Schuh (1996) is to contribute to the academic enterprise and to meet the institution's needs for basic services.

On a more practical level, student affairs divisions are being asked by their critics if their services and programs are essential and worthy of funding (Mayhew, Ford, and Hubbard, 1990). If the services they provide do not contribute to the success of the institution, then they may be dropped or considered for privatization. Even if services and programs are considered essential, questions regarding quality must still be answered. Assessment helps student affairs professionals make the connection between what they do and how they contribute to the institution's mission.

Assessment's Role

Chaffee and Sherr (1992, p. 1) state that although higher education professionals are for quality, the bigger question for many people is whether we actually "do" quality; assessment helps educators answer this question. We adopt Upcraft and Shuh's (1996) definition of assessment: "Assessment [is] any effort to gather, analyze, and interpret evidence that describes institutional, departmental, divisional, or agency effectiveness" (p. 18). This definition covers a variety of areas and is not limited to student learning outcomes; it includes program and source evaluation, needs analysis, student satisfaction, and so on, and applies to the institution's total effort (all component parts of the institution) whether it be academic affairs, student affairs, business affairs, university advancement, or other institutional concerns.

Assessment has been used by student affairs to determine student needs, student satisfaction, and to make judgments about the effectiveness of services and programs. Efforts have also been made to use assessment to understand the campus environment and to compare student services and outcomes at different institutions (benchmarking). Finally, student affairs departments have used assessment to measure effectiveness of functional work areas against professional standards (Council for the Advancement of Standards (CAS), 1986). Through assessment strategies, student affairs administrators are able to demonstrate that services and programs affect the desired outcomes of the institutions, that services and programs are essential to the institution, and that student affairs is able to show continued improvement in its services and programs over time.

Assessment, TQM, and Student Affairs

Assessment is not a new issue for student affairs and is an important part of TQM. Student affairs professionals want to satisfy customers (student, parents, and the institution) with the level and variety of services offered while promoting student development concepts and student learning in the framework of those services and programs. Student affairs professionals use assessment to measure student outcomes and the level of service extended through student satisfaction assessment tools. Through assessment, they try to show how student affairs programs and activities support institutional effectiveness; at the same time, they must assess how their programs and services contribute to the desired outcomes expected by students.

Whether educators like it or not, individuals and groups outside higher education are asking them to confirm that colleges and universities are delivering their promised product: education (Terenzini, 1989). Educators answer their external customers by using assessment to measure student outcomes and improvements in educational effectiveness. Likewise, student affairs educators are being asked how they contribute to desired student outcomes and educational effectiveness. Again, assessment aids student affairs professionals in deciding how they help the institution and how they can make ongoing efforts to improve services and programs that serve the institution. With increasing pressure for quality and accountability, it is difficult for student affairs professionals to know what areas of assessment and TQM to embrace.

Assessment in Student Affairs

Upcraft and Schuh (1996) took nine principles of good practice for assessing student learning (Hutchings and others, 1993) and adapted them to the assessment of student affairs. A discussion of the adaptation of these principles and their application to quality and TQM in student affairs follows.

PRINCIPLE 1: *"The assessment of student affairs begins with educational values"* (p. 22).

The most important institutional goals are the ones that are closely linked to the institution's overall educational mission. Educators must test or assess programs, activities, or services that they believe will make an institution more effective. Student affairs staff must constantly assess their programs and services to learn if they are successfully promoting student affairs values.

There are important goals within TQM, such as continuous quality improvement (CQI), employee empowerment, integrity, and so on; however, most formal TQM assessment involves changes made to a process for quality improvement. There have been few efforts at formally assessing the development of values within a TQM organization. There has been greater reliance on leadership and training to emphasize desired values within the TQM movement. For example, W. E. Deming's first TQM principle emphasizes "constancy of purpose for improvement of product and service," but it does not emphasize values. In Deming's model, TQM seeks to measure how the customer (in this case, the student) feels about the staff in residence halls as students move in and how this reflects on perceptions of service in the residence halls, but TQM would not necessarily seek to measure the resident staff's role in promoting self-discipline and developing a sense of community as a value.

PRINCIPLE 2: *"Assessment is most effective when it reflects an understanding of organizational outcomes as multidimensional, integrated, and revealed in performance over time"* (p. 22).

This statement reminds us that there are many parts to the organizational puzzle that contribute in a variety of ways to a desired outcome. The recognition of this complexity is important in determining how to appropriately assess the organization.

TQM is very compatible with this principle because it achieves its goals by looking at the key processes of an organization and how they help the organization achieve its purposes. For instance, TQM might use various charts, graphs, and methods to outline how students register for classes to fully understand that process. Then recommendations would be made for changes in how students register in order to improve the process. Finally TQM would use assessment to ask students if the registration process was actually improved.

By examining and assessing key processes in a student affairs division, staff can both improve their services and programs and also incrementally and continuously affect the outcomes of an entire institution. Assessment of programs and services helps staff to determine just how effective they are in contributing to an institution's mission. By doing this repeatedly over time, staff not only adhere to good principles of assessment but also promote CQI.

PRINCIPLE 3: *"Assessment works best when it has clear, explicitly stated goals"* (p. 23).

Simply put, the clearer institutional goals can be stated, the easier the assessment of whether those goals have been achieved. Usually, the clarity of a goal statement suggests what must be measured (or how to assess).

TQM emphasizes the need not only for a vision of what an institution hopes to become but also for a mission statement outlining the purpose of the institution (Hutton, 1994). TQM strives to assess changes in the key processes that promote an organization's mission; it also promotes stating changes in clear measurable terms. TQM would not, for example, allow for a goal that reads, "Our college hopes to change its image as a suitcase college by offering more weekend activities." Rather, TQM would restate the goal in a different manner: "By offering two major events each semester, the college hopes to keep more students on campus during weekends." This goal can now be measured and can provide feedback for improvement.

Student affairs, as stated earlier, must articulate in a clear manner just how it can help an institution achieve its mission. Erwin (1991) suggests that each student affairs unit should have a clear mission statement that specifies the particular learning objectives it hopes to promote and how it will assess its objectives.

PRINCIPLE 4: *"Assessment requires attention to outcomes but also, and just as important, to the processes that lead to them"* (p. 23).

TQM emphasizes that changes in quality come through continuous changes in the processes of an organization (Juran, 1989). This is congruent with Upcraft and Schuh's (1996) principle. If the focus is only on outcomes and not on how programs affect desired outcomes, then there is difficulty in improving or achieving the same outcomes over time. For example, an institutional goal or outcome might be improvement of student retention between the first and second years. TQM assesses this goal by looking at retention figures from each year as part of Deming's constancy-of-purpose principle. Of more importance in a TQM model would be what key process changes took place to improve retention rates. Thus TQM might assess the orientation or advisement of incoming first year students by looking at how the orientation or advisement process was altered and what effect it had on retention.

Student affairs departments generally use a variety of assessment techniques to determine how their programs and services affect the entire campus effort. Since the early 1970s, student development programs have increasingly used assessment tools. Now data exists to support how we contribute to an institution's goals through various activities, programs, and services.

PRINCIPLE 5: *"Assessment works best when it is ongoing, not episodic"* (p. 23).

As expected, one assessment done sporadically adds very little to the legitimacy of any program. Tracking progress of a program over time lends credibility to the results of program assessment.

TQM focuses on continuous improvement. If measurements or assessments are not done with each change in a process, it becomes impossible to verify that continuous improvement is ongoing. Many of the goals of student development and learning that student affairs professionals seek to implement can only be viewed over time. Without ongoing assessment, the effects of changes to specific programs and services would be difficult to determine. Fortunately, student affairs divisions in recent times have typically done well in the ongoing assessment of student satisfaction with services, programs, and staff response to their needs. A philosophy of continuous improvement is readily acceptable in the student affairs culture.

PRINCIPLE 6: *"Assessment is most effective when representatives from across student affairs and the institution are involved"* (p. 23).

By including others in assessment efforts, student affairs not only improves those efforts, but engenders a greater understanding of student affairs values, mission, and vision with the campus in general. For example, members from all areas of the campus involved in orientation (faculty, academic administrators, business affairs staff, student affairs professionals, students, etc.) should be included in the review of this key process. This cross-functional team would recommend those changes to the orientation program that would make it a better process for students and parents. These recommendations could only be made after in-depth discussions and consensus from various areas of the campus represented on the team. Ultimately an assessment of the new changes to orientation would be a part of the TQM technique. The learning that took place among members of the cross-functional team because of the discussion of the orientation process is reflected in Upcraft and Schuh's sixth principle. The fact that others from around the campus were involved in making the changes to orientation only strengthens their view of orientation and the results of the assessment.

This principle illustrates the need for student affairs to establish its programs in conjunction with both the customers (students) and stakeholders in order to increase the credibility of assessment results and increasing quality of services.

PRINCIPLE 7: *"Assessment makes a difference when it begins with issues of use and illuminates questions that people really care about"* (p. 24).

Educators often keep an abundance of statistics, charts, and surveys that relate very little to what may be considered important. For example, if a president or chancellor questioned the level of student activity on their campus and student affairs staff quickly assembled charts, graphs, and statistics showing how many programs had been implemented with attendance figures over the past several months, what would this illustrate? The important information is not how many programs are offered and not how many students attended different events but rather the average student's satisfaction level with what was offered and the overall quality of the programs.

TQM methods are compatible with this principle because TQM emphasizes making changes to those key processes that will greatly affect the customer and thus reflect on the institution.

PRINCIPLE 8: *"Assessment should be part of a larger set of conditions that promote change"* (p. 24).

Assessment is no substitute for leadership in an ongoing effort to improve student services and programs. Assessment simply helps us to know if we are on the right track. How assessment is used is what really counts.

Seymour (1992, p. 15) says that "there is no substitute for leadership when it comes to quality." There may be many areas in student affairs on a campus involved in assessment but it is leadership that focuses those assessment efforts into something meaningful for both student affairs and the institution. It is also leadership that approves the changes to key processes and empowers people to make changes outlined as key elements of TQM.

As mentioned earlier in this chapter, student affairs must contribute to the student outcomes expected by the institution and at the same time must improve essential services such as housing, health services, counseling, and so on. This is not a new idea for student affairs professionals who recognize that at any given moment the cleanliness or level of noise of a residence hall may be far more important to students, parents, and administrators than another long-range student outcome. TQM emphasizes that leadership is still necessary to determine what is important at a given time.

One of the lessons for student affairs is that although we believe we make a significant contribution to student learning and the educational outcomes sought by the institution, we are often judged on the simple results of the daily services we render.

PRINCIPLE 9: *"Through assessment, student affairs professionals meet responsibilities of students, the institution, and the public"* (p. 24).

Assessment is a means to an end. It gives us the information required to show what and how we are assisting with institutional effectiveness. By offering the best services and programs, we help students, the institution, and the public.

TQM uses its goal of continuous improvement as a way of offering services and programs that satisfy the needs of customers and stakeholders. Assessing customer and stakeholder satisfaction determines if continuous improvement is occurring and if quality is improving.

Conclusion

Student affairs departments and professionals are being held accountable by the public and by many governmental agencies for the quality of higher-education institutions. At another level, students are asking for more in terms of services and programs considering the tuition and fees they pay. Furthermore, educators are being asked to prove that what they are offering is worthy of support.

With increasing pressures for accountability and improvement, many institutions are considering a variety of strategies to show progress. TQM is one way to address the many issues facing higher education. Using assessment is another way of responding to questions of improvement and accountability. The difference is that TQM methods may help us to achieve our goals if properly implemented and embraced. But nothing will be achieved if we cannot demonstrate that we are becoming more effective organizations. This evidence can only come through assessment.

References

Alexander, L., Clinton, B., and Kean, T. H. *Time for Results: The Governors' 1991 Report on Education.* Washington, D.C.: National Governors' Association, 1986.

Chaffee, E., and Sherr, L. *Quality: Transforming Postsecondary Education.* ASHE-ERIC Higher Education Report no. 3. Washington, D.C.: School of Education and Human Development, George Washington University, 1992.

Council for the Advancement of Standards for Student Services/Development Programs. *CAS Standards and Guidelines for Student Services/Development Programs.* Washington, D.C.: Council for the Advancement of Standards, 1986.

Erwin, T. D. *Assessing Student Learning and Development: A Guide to the Principles, Goals, and Methods of Determining College Outcomes.* San Francisco: Jossey-Bass, 1991.

Hanson, G. "The Call to Assessment: What Role for Student Affairs?" In K. J. Beeler and D. E. Hunter (eds.), *Puzzles and Pieces in Wonderland: The Promise and Practice of Student Affairs*

Research. Washington, D.C.: National Association of Student Personnel Administrators, 1991.

Hutchings, P., and others. "Principles of Good Practice for Assessing Student Learning." *Assessment Update,* 1993, *5* (1), 6–7.

Hutton, D. W. *The Change Agents Handbook.* Milwaukee, Wis.: ASQC Quality Press, 1994.

Juran, J. M. *Juran on Leadership for Quality.* New York: Free Press, 1989.

Marchese, T. J. "Assessment's Next Five Years." *Association of Institutional Research Newsletter* (special supplement), Fall–Winter 1990, pp. 1–4.

Mayhew, L. B., Ford, P. J., and Hubbard, D. L. *The Quest for Quality: The Challenge for Undergraduate Education in the 1990s.* San Francisco: Jossey-Bass, 1990.

Seymour, D. T. *On Q: Causing Quality in Higher Education.* New York: Macmillan, 1992.

Southern Regional Education Board. "Access to Quality Undergraduate Education." *Chronicle of Higher Education,* July 3, 1985, pp. 9–12.

Terenzini, P. T. "Assessment with Open Eyes: Pitfalls in Studying Student Outcomes." *Journal of Higher Education,* 1989, *60* (6), 644–664.

Upcraft, M. L., and Schuh, J. H. *Assessment in Student Affairs: A Guide for Practitioners.* San Francisco: Jossey-Bass, 1996.

RICHARD M. SCOTT *is assistant vice chancellor for business affairs at the University of North Carolina at Wilmington. He served seven years as a student affairs professional and is a former president of the National Association of College Auxiliary Services.*

Total quality management does not adequately address leadership, vision, purpose, organizational culture, motivation, and change. These aspects of organizational life are better described by the learning organization model.

What TQM Does Not Address

Curt Kochner, Timothy R. McMahon

As shown in previous chapters, total quality management (TQM) has been used successfully in many ways and at many different institutions of higher education. Like any other management tool or model, it offers insight into the process of how something happens—whether it is the analysis of what occurs once a prospective student writes an institution for an admission application or how rooms are assigned in residence halls. Whether the quality improvement model used is Deming's (1986), Crosby's (1979), or Juran's (1988), in essence it is a process model—it helps an organization do something better. However, TQM does not encourage (force?) an organization to examine its efforts to improve what it should be doing. In other words, TQM helps an organization make better widgets but it does not help an organization determine if making widgets is what it should be doing.

This chapter explores the importance of leadership, vision, purpose, organizational culture, motivation, and change as aspects of organizational life that TQM does not adequately address. Finally, the concept of learning organizations is offered as a needed additional element in the leadership and management discussion.

The Importance of Leadership, Vision, Purpose, Organizational Culture, Motivation, and Change

Total quality management programs naturally focus attention on the topics of internal management, maximizing production, increasing the financial bottom line, improvement of service, creating a culture dedicated to efficiency, motivating employees by creating commitment to the team efforts, and changing the organization through proven principles. All these objectives are designed to help the organization increase quality of services and fiscal growth.

Programs that focus on improving the management of an organization will often miss some larger issues such as leadership, vision as a global concept, how corporate purpose affects individuals' sense of meaning, implications of an organization's interactions with external cultures, motivation of employees as individuals rather than as members of a team, and change as a participative rather than a directive process. By ignoring these critical aspects of organizational (and human) life, the true success of any program will be limited.

Leadership. One of the most important concepts that TQM does not address is the role of the leader in the organization. The leader, as defined in TQM literature, is seen as a persuasive supervisor who efficiently helps the team maximum performance. This limits the role, responsibility, and expectations of the leader when compared to how the leader's role is conceptualized in other related literature. Deming's (1994) description of leadership focuses on the leader's ability to "accomplish transformation of his organization. He possesses knowledge, personality, and persuasive power" (p. 116). The leader is portrayed as a motivator with the ability to clearly communicate a well-defined plan and mobilize a team to succeed. "It is a leader's job to foster joy in work, harmony, and teamwork" (Aguayo, 1991, p. 181). Although these are attributes of leadership, Deming expects the leader to focus on the internal efficiency of the organization. TQM principles are naturally designed to improve the management and efficiency of the organization and do not focus on the external environment.

As Walton notes in *The Deming Management Method* (1986), the term *supervisor* has been interchanged with *leader.* "The job of the supervisor is not to tell people what to do or to punish them but to lead. Leading consists of helping people do a better job and of learning by objective methods who is in need of individual help" (p. 35). Further, in noting this distinction, Aguayo (1991) states, "since my first encounter with Deming, he has substituted the word *leadership* for *supervision*" (p. 176).

The leadership responsibility of adapting to external changes and setting new and innovative directions for an organization is generally overlooked in the TQM literature. The flexibility and creativity to see new goals and directions for the organization, based on clear knowledge of the company's role in the larger marketplace, are often lost as the organization strives to improve the existing paradigm. Those who are successful in providing leadership are required to take a role beyond motivating employees to perform more efficiently. For example, a company making "zero-tolerance" eight-track tapes may have excellent application of TQM principles, but is clearly not receiving adequate leadership.

Other writers have framed leadership in a manner different from the TQM perspective. Gardner notes in *On Leadership* (1990) that "the first thing that strikes one as characteristic of contemporary leadership is the necessity for the leader to work with and through extremely complex organizations and institutions—corporations, government agencies at all levels, the courts, the media of communication, and so on. Leaders must understand not only the intricate organizational patterns of their own segment but also the workings of neighboring segments" (p. 81). This definition has a spirit of connectedness to a larger, external and complex system rather than an internal focus on efficiency presented in TQM models. Similarly, as Bennis and Nanus (1985) note in *Leaders: The Strategies That Take Charge,* and as Nanus (1989) further articulates in *The Leader's Edge:* "Managers are concerned with doing things right. Deeply involved in the process of running their organizations, they are responsible for guiding operations so that they are conducted efficiently, at minimum cost, and on schedule. Leaders care about these things too, but they concentrate on effectiveness rather than efficiency. They focus on doing the right thing and on choosing what should be done and why, not just how to do it. They are more deeply involved in the total direction of the organization rather than in process, making sure that the organization is doing what it should be doing to earn legitimacy, its future access to resources, and its strengths, growth, and long-term survivability"(pp. 47–48).

Additionally, the concepts of *servant leadership* (Greenleaf, 1977; Spears, 1995) and *Leader as Steward* (Block, 1993) are not part of the interpretation of leadership offered by Deming and others in the TQM movement. The idea of viewing the leader as a steward who helps create a liberating vision in an organization that is seen as very similar to a tightly knit community seems miles away from the description of leadership as offered by TQM proponents.

Finally, the world of Deming, Crosby, and Juran is certainly a Newtonian world—made up of parts begging to be managed and controlled. Other writers (Beckhard and Pritchard, 1992; Gleick, 1987; Goldstein, 1995; Kellert, 1993; Kelly, 1994; McGill and Slocum, 1994; Mitroff and Linstone, 1993; Stacey, 1992; Wheatley, 1992) have noted that the real world is more chaotic in nature—a world of wholes, not parts, in which order exists but is often difficult to see. Most importantly, it is a world that understands that control is not possible, so leaders must work to shape the behaviors of those they are trying to lead.

Vision. The concepts of vision and mission are seldom mentioned in the TQM literature. When vision is addressed, as in *The Five Pillars of TQM* by Bill Creech (1994), it is limited to the importance of pursuing a vision of TQM implementation. Vision is not seen as a guiding force of leadership but as a management tool. Vision as an important concept has been overlooked by TQM. The importance of vision and mission have been stressed by many authors including Albrecht (1994), Collins and Porras (1994), and Senge (1992). Wheatley (1992) went so far as to note that "we need to be able to trust that something as simple as a clear core set of values and vision, kept in motion through continuing dialogue, can lead to order" (p. 147). Without a vision shared throughout the organization, empowerment can lead to stronger, more capable individuals moving in many different directions at the same time resulting in little true movement for an entire organization (Senge, 1992).

The ability to determine how the organization fits into the world around it, and how and why the future will affect what the organization will do are a part of vision. TQM generally limits its focus on how the organization will improve its current practices and enhance productivity. Again, Gardner (1990) offers some wise words on this topic: "Of the popularly expressed requirements for leadership, one of the most common is that leaders have vision, which can mean a variety of things: that they think long-term; that they see where their system fits in a larger context; that they can describe the outlines of a possible future that lifts and moves people; or that they actually discern, in the clutter and confusion of the present, the elements that determine what is to come" (pp. 130–131).

The principles of TQM are not designed to address the "what" and "why" questions about products or services of the organization, they focus instead on how to improve production and efficiency of any existing product or service. As Richards (1995) notes, "creating a vision is an artist's act of deciding both what is to be made and why it is to be made, whether the thing is a product, process, company, or manufacturing plant" (p. 108). Words even remotely similar to this do not appear in Deming's fourteen points or in the related TQM literature.

Purpose. The first of Deming's fourteen points is to "create constancy of purpose toward improvement of product and service" (1986, p. 23). "Establishing constancy of purpose means (1) innovation; (2) research and education; (3) continuous improvement of product and service; (4) maintenance of equipment, furniture, and fixtures, and new aids to production in the office and in the plant" (Walton, p. 56). Although constancy of purpose focuses on improving a known product, it draws attention to the present and the internal rather than to the future and the external. TQM does not address issues of the soul and spirit of the workplace, other than noting the importance of driving fear out of the workplace. But even when TQM addresses the issue of fear in the workplace, it is limited to removing employee fear of admitting mistakes or fear of making suggestions for change. The strong connection between product, production, and process may keep the organization from addressing the larger issue of meaning. This could potentially be a fatal mistake if the organization does not have a clear understanding of why it does what it does or if it fails to recognize the global results of its work.

Focusing on the concept of purpose as it relates to a product or services also keeps us from seeing purpose as a concept that includes finding meaning in our individual lives from a spiritual viewpoint. Bolman and Deal (1995) warn educators about the drawbacks of pursuing only the improvement of efficiency and the bottom line. "When we succumb to greed, focus only on the bottom line, and worship exclusively at the altar of rationality, we undermine our search for meaning, passion, and a sense of life's deeper, spiritual purpose" (p. 164). This idea of purpose is much different from the "constancy of purpose" emphasized in TQM. As Chittister (1990) notes, "the problem is that we must learn to distinguish between purpose and meaning in life. Purpose has something to do with being productive and setting goals and knowing what needs to be done and doing it. It is easy to have purpose. To write seven letters today, to wax that floor, to finish this legal brief, to make out those reports, to complete this degree, that's purpose. Meaning, on the other hand, depends on my asking myself who will care and who will profit and who will be touched and who will be forgotten or hurt or affected by my doing those things. Purpose determines what I will do with this part of my life. Meaning demands to know why I'm doing it and with what global results" (p. 102). Fulghum, in his essay entitled "Pay Attention" (1995), also discusses the importance of spiritual issues. He notes that "'nourishing the soul' means making sure I attend to those things that give my life richness and depth of meaning" (p. 10).

TQM principles focus on improvement of the corporate financial bottom line. These principles do not address matters of the personal lives of employees, such as how the employees' work contributes to their sense of integrity, significance, personal vision, emotional safety, and personal sense of purpose and depth of meaning. If we are to address the matter of purpose in a more personal manner, we may look to the work of Peter Senge in *The Fifth Discipline* (1992). The discipline of personal mastery involves "a process of continually focusing and refocusing on what one truly wants, on one's vision" (p. 149). Senge addresses the importance of having a personal vision and purpose to direct our efforts. He states that "when we are unclear between interim goals and more intrinsic goals, the subconscious has no way of prioritizing and focusing" (Senge, 1992, p. 165). He sees important connections between the personal purposes of individuals and how these are brought together for a corporate vision and purpose.

TQM teaches the organization to constantly focus on the improvement of product and service. It does not, however, encourage individuals in the organization to constantly focus on things that bring their "life richness and depth of meaning," as Fulghum states, nor does TQM invite the individual to participate in "a process of continually focusing and refocusing on what one truly wants, on one's vision," as Senge states (1992, p. 149). In looking at what TQM does not address, the matter of personal purpose, sense of meaning, and passion cannot be overlooked.

Culture. The organizational culture that TQM strives to develop is one of teamwork and excellence in performance. It is a culture that supports individuals in admitting mistakes and invites suggestions for improvements. Finally, the culture is one that strives for continuous improvement, or *kaizen,* focuses on increasing the bottom line, and maintains a relentless pursuit of quality. "Quality must become the new religion" (Walton, 1986, p. 58). Although these are certainly admirable goals, the attainment of these goals is rooted in material measurements, specifically the bottom-line numbers. The culture will naturally be most concerned about the organization's internal, financial, and material matters.

There is an old leadership principle that states, "If you want it, measure it. If you can't measure it, forget it." Deming's foundations for TQM are based on statistical measures and increases in quality are determined through the measurement of production. However, some essential components and values important to the development of the culture may be absent if the organization only focuses on what it can measure.

An organization that forgets those aspects that it cannot measure will tend to overlook soul and spirit issues such as significance, community, creativity, intuition, integrity, honesty, risk-taking, self-esteem, personal sense of purpose and meaning, diversity, nurturing of the spirit, and emotional safety. An organization that recognizes and nurtures these matters will create a culture that is much different from the culture created by a TQM-oriented team that is constantly striving to improve product and service. Bolman and Deal (1995) present a clear picture of the differences between these two organizational cultures in *Leading with Soul*: "Maybe your head and hands have taken you as far as they can. Consider a new route. A journey of the heart. Your heart is more than a pump. It's your spiritual center. Heart is courage and compassion. Without it life is empty, lonely. You're always busy but never fulfilled" (p. 25).

A TQM-guided organization will create a very efficient "pump," and it will also expect that employees will be fulfilled through their participation in a successful group effort. Bolman and Deal (1995) suggest, however, that a culture like this does not address some crucial personal matters. Although TQM strives to create a specific culture based on teamwork and efficiency, it does not address the deeper and unmeasurable issues of heart, soul, and spirit. It is very possible for employees in an organization embracing the principles of TQM to be "always busy but never fulfilled."

Schein (1992) offers another framework for analyzing organizational culture by noting that three levels of culture exist in organizations: artifacts, espoused values, and basic underlying assumptions. Artifacts are the most easily observed aspects of culture and include virtually anything that is visible within an organizational environment, including organizational structure and processes. Espoused values include the strategies, goals, and philosophies embraced by the organization. Finally, the basic underlying assumptions are the unconscious beliefs, perceptions, thoughts, and feelings that exist within the organization. It is in this layer that the true sources of the organization's values and actions are found.

Schein's model is useful in helping us better understand how an organization works. The organization's basic underlying assumptions and values drive the strategies, goals, and philosophy, resulting in a purposeful organization structure and set of processes. For an organization that has at its core a set of values that supports TQM, a certain set of processes will result. As has been noted earlier, these processes will focus on teamwork, excellence, continuous improvement, and on increasing the bottom line. This is very different from an organization that has at its core a set of values that supports the development of soul and spirit in the workplace. In such an environment, the belief exists that the bottom line will take care of itself as long as the basic human needs of the organization's members are met, including having a sense that their work is purposeful and meaningful.

Motivation. The motivation for persons working in a TQM-oriented environment will emanate from the successes of the organization. Deming did not see value in using material or monetary incentives for rewarding improvement of quality. He believed that a quality employee stayed in an organization because he liked a work setting that provided an opportunity for him "to use his knowledge for the benefit of the whole system. He takes joy in his work" (Deming, 1994, p. 114). The focus of motivation is the achievement of excellence by the organization.

The success of the organization will be based on bottom-line successes, and TQM teaches that financial success will be attainable through improved structures, controls, and procedures. The primary motivation that TQM relies upon is internal—expecting that individual employees will experience joy from being a part of the team that has achieved higher quality performance. Dick Richards in *Artful Work* (1995) also addresses the importance of joy in the organization. He writes, "Joy arrives on the wings of discovery and surprise. It inhabits us when we excel. Joy is not a goal of artful work but the result of doing something challenging and doing it well—so well that the doing leads us into realms we did not expect. We surprise ourselves. Joy occurs when we transcend who we think we are and what we think we are capable of creating" (p. 38). The major difference here is the source of the joy. The joy that one might feel from being a part of making the organization run more efficiently is different than the joy one feels from experiencing personal growth beyond what we thought we could do or be. The source of the joy Deming describes is from corporate success. The joy that Richards describes is from personal growth and success. TQM does not address the value of the motivation that comes from personal victories, but relies on individuals being motivated through their participation as members of the team.

In *Leading with Soul*, Bolman and Deal discuss the importance of *significance* as a motivating factor. They contend that we bring soul and spirit into the workplace when we provide opportunities for individuals to feel significant. "Significance comes from working with others, doing something worth doing, making the world better" (p. 96). Although there is the component of working with others in a team setting, much like a TQM model, there is a key difference. "Doing something worth doing, making the world better" may mean something more significant than improving the bottom-line of the organization—the primary goal of TQM.

Change. Dr. Deming suggested that changes be made in the management systems in the United States as early as 1950. His ideas for change were rejected until they were proven successful in Japan, and it was only in the 1980s that the concepts of TQM became acceptable and popular in this country. It is ironic that the reasons for the rejection of Deming's ideas may have been due to the style by which he suggested change rather than the substance of his ideas.

Considering that the management ideas of Deming were so revolutionary and effective, why did the management community in the United States take so long to embrace the concepts? In *Leading Change*, James O'Toole (1995) explores why Deming was rejected in the United States for so long: "When Deming first dealt with the Japanese, he listened to them, showed them respect, and couched his ideas in terms of their needs. But later, when he came to deal with Americans, he was imperious and arrogantly demanded that they swallow his philosophy whole" (p. 198).

The answer may be in a very fundamental understanding of the process of change. Bridges (1991) describes the process of change as having three stages: beginnings, endings, and a neutral zone. The neutral zone is where we live in uncertainty and confusion and determines our future direction. Deming did not invite American management into a neutral zone where they could buy into the concepts of TQM. His convictions and certainty about the concepts of TQM led him to attempt to move management from the old to the new without the benefit of time in the neutral zone of uncertainty where they could come to understand and accept the concepts on their terms.

TQM does not address change in the same manner described by Bridges (1991) or as Peter Senge (1992) outlines in *The Fifth Discipline*. Bridges sees change as providing endings, neutral zones, and beginnings; Senge sees change as consisting of current reality and a future vision—through creative tension organizations move from where they are (current reality) to where they want to be (future vision).

TQM does not recognize or honor the complexity of the change process. The principles of TQM are presented as a recipe, certain to move an organization to a new way of operating. True change involves more than a change in behavior. It also involves a new way of thinking. New ways of thinking emerge from involvement in the change process, sharing of individual goals and aspirations, listening, dialogue, and development of a shared vision.

The Learning Organization—A Different Approach

Peter Senge (1992) and others (Senge and others, 1994) have developed the idea of a learning organization as a concept that captures much of what is missing in the TQM movement. With its emphasis on mental models, personal mastery, team learning, shared vision, and systems thinking, these authors have created a framework that offers an organization a new perspective from which to operate. This new perspective stresses the importance of learning and of establishing mechanisms within the organization to continuously make learning a priority.

As Garvin describes, "A learning organization is an organization skilled at creating, acquiring, and transferring knowledge, and at modifying its behavior to reflect new knowledge and insights" (1993, p. 80). Although this may sound like much in the TQM literature, there is a major difference. The TQM strategy focuses almost exclusively on "single-loop learning." A certain set of processes produces a certain set of results. These results are analyzed using TQM tools and the processes are changed to produce more or better results. Argyris and

Schön (1974) developed an idea called "double-loop learning", which was later expanded by Argyris (1993). In this model, a set of assumptions or beliefs cause a set of processes to be developed that produce a set of results. In order for the results to become better, both the processes and the set of underlying assumptions and beliefs must be examined. Because TQM relies solely on single-loop learning, it never gets to the assumptions or beliefs of an organization—its mission or vision; the critical issue of "why we exist" is never asked. With the importance of having a shared vision being stressed by the learning organization model, it offers a different and very vital perspective for organizations.

Aspects of the Learning Organization. Senge (1992) articulates five aspects of the learning organization: mental models, personal mastery, team learning, shared vision, and systems thinking. In this section, these aspects will be described and their relevance to student affairs and higher education further developed. Although other descriptions of learning organizations exist and should be reviewed (Garvin, 1993; Kline and Saunders, 1993; Marquardt and Reynolds, 1994; Swieringa and Wierdsma, 1992; Useem and Kochan, 1992; Watkins and Marsick, 1993), Senge's work offers a very understandable, usable model from which to work.

Mental Models. Mental models are the combined set of thoughts, beliefs, and assumptions that we make about a concept. For example, what comes to mind when you hear the words *budget process* or *professional development?* Contrast your reaction with hearing the word *dorm* as opposed to hearing the preferred term *residence hall.* We all have this set of thoughts, beliefs, and assumptions in our brains and it is based on our experiences, knowledge, and opinions. The problem, as Senge and others (1994) have described, is that many of these mental models are hard to reach because they are buried so deep inside us. If they cannot be unearthed, they cannot be examined. If they cannot be examined, they cannot be changed. Consequently, it is important to understand our mental models.

Today many of our mental models are being challenged. We are asked to consider if a group of students or staff connected only by computer lines and similar interests can be called a community. In student development theory, we are told that we need to go far beyond the traditional theorists, Chickering, Perry, and Kohlberg, to include the work of Belenky, Clinchy, Goldberger, and Tarule (1986); Gilligan, Cross, Helms, Cass, and many more. Our ideas about leadership are challenged by authors who embrace the chaos perspective—that leaders must be facilitators of disorder, not caretakers of order (Wheatley, 1992). The impact of technology, science, and changing demographics is causing our mental models to be challenged on a regular basis. Knowing what we think we know and recognizing what we do not know will become even more important skills in the learning organization. Finally, mental models are important in what we expect from work. Is work something one does to pay the bills or is work more of a vocation or calling? Answers to these questions can drive what people want and need from a work environment.

Mental models exist in the minds of members of organizations whether the organizations embrace TQM or not. But the models will differ based on the prevailing philosophy of the particular organization. Imagine being a member of an organization that embraces the TQM philosophy and hearing the term *organizational mission*. Your mind would probably conjure up a mental image of a group or team of individuals striving for efficiency and for doing things in the most expedient manner. Now imagine the same term from the perspective of someone whose organization embraces as its core values the concepts of spirit, soul, integrity, significance, community, creativity, intuition, risk-taking, self-esteem, personal sense of purpose and meaning, and diversity. Two sets of mental models exist—each very different from the other, yet both equally hard to identify because they are so ingrained. What we are trying to accomplish, organizationally, will eventually become part of who we are as human beings. It is important for us to be aware of our mental models because they influence everything we do, sometimes without us even knowing it.

Questions to ask ourselves include the following: What do I know? How do I know this to be true? Are there other possible explanations? What additional insights might these other explanations provide?

Personal Mastery. Personal mastery means working continuously to do things better. Much of the success of any organization is tied to this idea. The phrase "work smarter, not harder" has become overused recently, but it does provide some basis for improving, on an individual basis, how things are accomplished. In times of decreasing budgets, this obviously becomes increasingly important, yet we sometimes miss a critical element in our discussions of helping ourselves and others be more productive. We have moved from "do more with less" to "do different with less." This makes sense, but believing that more can be demanded of fewer and fewer staff members will eventually destroy an organization. Imagine, however, if this is taken one step further. From "do different with less" to "do different with more," but it's a different kind of "more." Ask the question, "What do we have more of now than we did five years ago?" Responses might include more technology, more knowledgeable staff members, more diversity, and more information about what conditions foster student learning. Using this information to work smarter is the key and adding to this information in a continuous, ongoing manner is a critical aspect of a learning organization.

Learning and mastery must take many forms—some of which we now use (for instance, professional reading and conferences, staff development sessions, and new staff orientation and training) and others that we do not use as much as we could (such as working collaboratively with faculty having similar interests, professional reading and conferences outside the field of student affairs, and reading and dialoguing about the same book as a staff). For too long, professional development has been equated largely with professional conferences. With rising costs, this may become a thing of the past, possibly replaced by video conferences.

Establishing an organizational culture that is conducive to learning on a daily basis through debate and discussion is more efficient than relying on periodic staff development sessions or professional conferences. In some ways, this culture is similar to the TQM principle of continuous improvement, except that what is being improved or increased are the knowledge and skills of the staff member. Increasing one's personal mastery—becoming more knowledgeable and skillful—is a necessity in any organization. In a TQM-oriented organization, this improvement is tied to developing a product in a better, more efficient way. In an organization embracing the concepts of soul and spirit, the improvement is more closely connected to individuals developing an enhanced sense of purpose in what they are doing. Questions to ask ourselves include: What do I need to learn? How can I learn it? Who can help me learn it?

Team Learning. Team learning includes the idea that in an organization there are some tasks that people do as individuals and there are other tasks that require people to do them as a team. This idea could include learning how to work more effectively on group projects or deciding how to meet together as a staff (how will you make decisions, work through disagreements, and deal with conflict, for example). The concept of teamwork has become overused and underappreciated in recent years with many leaders and managers claiming that their organizations are working as teams. Of course the reality, when the question is posed to line staff, is often the opposite; this concept is something that is easy to talk about and very difficult to do well.

We have all been members of well-intentioned workgroups composed of good staff members that simply did not live up to their potential. We have also been members of overachieving groups. What causes such discrepancies? The synergistic anthem of the whole being greater than the sum of its parts can be true, but only if we understand the concept of *andness.* One and one can equal two, or zero, or fifty based on the "and" that exists in the equation. If you disagree, imagine the staff member with whom you work the very best. The two of you can accomplish great things, much more than anyone could predict. In this case one and one equal much more than two. Now imagine that staff member with whom you do not connect. In this case, although you are both smart and full of good intentions, one and one often equals less than one.

Teams are an integral part of most organizations—those embracing TQM and those that do not. One of the key points to remember is that groups always need to learn how to work well together—it will not happen naturally, even if members have the best of intentions. Placing an emphasis on groups learning to do things together can help the organization accomplish amazing things. If significance, trust, community, creativity, intuition, integrity, honesty, risk-taking, self-esteem, personal sense of purpose and meaning, diversity, nurturing of the spirit, and emotional safety are truly aspects of organizational life, it is undoubtedly going to be easier to form the team initially, and to move the team to a level of high productivity more quickly.

Questions to ask ourselves include: What do we need to learn to do together as a team? How can we learn it? Who can help us learn it? What relationships are important in your organization? What relationships need to be strengthened in your organization? How do the policies, procedures, and structures of your organization help create and support relationships?

Shared Vision. Shared vision is the belief that an organization will only be successful when its individuals and teams are aligned and are working toward the same vision and mission. The importance of having a shared vision has already been articulated in this chapter. The relationship between having a shared vision and personal empowerment efforts is a crucial one and relates to the notion of personal mastery mentioned earlier. Personal empowerment or mastery without a shared vision creates stronger, more knowledgeable individuals, yet does little for the organization as a whole (Senge, 1990). This is such a powerful idea because it connects with the ideas of leadership, vision, purpose, organizational culture, and change—all concepts that TQM models lack. Without a shared vision, collective efforts have no shared goal, direction, or purpose. Having a shared vision encourages the development of synergistic relationships within the organization and helps individuals gain a sense of why the organization exists and how their roles contribute to making the organization better. It is only through having a shared vision that everyone in the organization can be, as Tom Peters (1994) says, in "the pursuit of wow!"

Questions to ask ourselves include: Why does your organization exist? What are your organizational values? What is your organizational culture? How does your culture support or detract from your mission? Is your mission statement known to all and used to guide behaviors and administrative decisions?

Systems Thinking. Systems thinking brings mental models, personal mastery, team learning, and shared vision together as it conceptualizes the organization as an entity in which everything literally influences everything else. Edward Lorenz (1993, p. 181) posed the following question in a 1972 presentation at the 139th meeting of the American Association for the Advancement of Science: "Predictability: Does the Flap of a Butterfly's Wings in Brazil Set Off a Tornado in Texas?" As he recently noted, "I avoided answering the question, but noted that if a single flap could lead to a tornado that would not otherwise have formed, it could equally well prevent a tornado that would otherwise have formed" (1993, p. 14). If a single flap of a butterfly's wings can affect the weather halfway across the globe, it makes sense that one staff member, incident, or policy can have an impact across an entire campus.

Certainly this is evident whenever a crisis or tragedy occurs on a campus—students, faculty, staff, and members of the community all feel the effects of such incidents. The impact of a person or incident is also evident when an occasion worthy of great celebration happens. But other examples exist in every organization because a campus is truly an interactive system. Consider the following examples: An institution hires a new adviser for its sororities and fraternities. This person has such a positive impact on the student leaders of the various chapters that it even reaches their chapter advisers and alumni. This person also influences the surrounding environment as the chapters become more involved in making a positive contribution to the local community. Finally, faculty also feel the impact as the Greek system begins to place more emphasis on academics. Some may argue that this is an idealistic example, yet the positive (or negative) impact that a single person can have on an entire campus community has been seen by everyone. Similarly, a single policy change can have far-reaching implications. What happens when an institution lowers (or raises) its admissions standards? Does it only impact the teaching faculty? Certainly not. Its impact is felt far beyond the boundaries of the classroom and extends into every aspect of life on campus and in the surrounding community.

Metaphors are powerful tools and Morgan (1986) provides some fascinating examples. For the purposes of this section, conceptualize how your organization is like a weather system. Words like stormy, sunny, unpredictable, cloudy, cold, hot, windy, and maybe even destructive probably come to mind. Contrast this with the images that come to mind when you conceptualize your organization as a machine. Different phrases, phrases like "made up of interchangeable parts," "when one part breaks down, you replace it," "needs fuel to run," "produces a product," "may need an occasional oil change" quickly come forth. The images people have when using the weather system metaphor are significantly different from the images they have when using the machine metaphor. The meteorological metaphor describes the quantum world of wholes—the whole is only understood by studying the whole system. The machine metaphor describes a Newtonian world of parts—study the parts and an understanding of the whole is surmised (Wheatley, 1992). Of course both perspectives offer a unique set of perspectives. Until recently, the machine metaphor has been used almost exclusively. The new paradigm suggests the necessity of also using the weather system metaphor.

Peter Senge (1992) introduced the idea of systems thinking as both a conceptualization and a set of tools that can be used to help people understand the complex interworkings of organizations. He noted that members of an organization and the causes of problems in the organization are part of a single system. It does no good, therefore, to blame others or outside circumstances for any difficulties being faced by the organization. The solutions to the problems being faced by the organization lie within the organization. Tools that have been developed to help others understand and use these concepts to uncover these solutions are described in detail in *The Fifth Discipline Fieldbook* (Senge and others, 1994), and include everything from exercises to help members of an organization construct a vision for their collective future to guidelines for how to create dialogue within a group.

Questions to ask ourselves include the following: How is your organization like a machine? How is your organization like a weather system? What aspects of your organization lend themselves to the machine metaphor? What aspects of your organization lend themselves to the weather system metaphor? What patterns, rhythms, and flows exist in your organization? What events occurring outside your organization are causing problems within it?

The Leader in the Learning Organization. Peter Senge (1990) identifies three roles for the leader in the learning organization: designer, teacher, and steward. As a designer, the leader helps the members of the organization build a foundation of purpose and core values and then tries to translate these ideas into actual decisions. As a teacher, the leader helps everyone understand what is really happening in and around the organization—its current reality—and helps members understand their own mental models. As a steward, the leader helps members feel that they are a part of a purpose larger than themselves. It is obvious that this kind of leader has a strong connection to the concepts of vision and purpose.

Conclusion

The purpose of this chapter has been to highlight those critical elements of organizational life that seem to be missing from the TQM model. Although TQM has much to offer as a process model and, to some degree, as a management tool, it lacks adequate conceptualizations of leadership, vision, purpose, organizational culture, motivation, and change. The authors believe that the model of learning organizations offered by Senge and others (1994) seems to offer much of what is lacking in the TQM perspective. As with any theoretical construct, its success as a model for actual practice will be more directly related to the quality of efforts of those trying to implement it than it will be to the quality of the model itself. Sometimes lost in our hurry to embrace the newest management trend is the idea that any framework on which people would like to base the future of their organization must involve some very basic requirements—that we tell the truth, that we value the dignity and contribution of every member of the organization, and that we have the courage, both individually and organizationally, to ask the tough questions of ourselves and of the organization. Only by doing these things will our organizations be able to meet the challenges they are facing today and will face tomorrow.

References

Aguayo, R. *Dr. Deming.* New York: Simon & Schuster, 1991.

Albrecht, K. *The Northbound Train.* New York: AMACOM, 1994.

Argyris, C. *Knowledge for Action: A Guide for Overcoming Barriers to Organizational Change.* San Francisco: Jossey-Bass, 1993.

Argyris, C., and Schön, D. A. *Theory in Practice: Increasing Professional Effectiveness.* San Francisco: Jossey-Bass, 1974.

Beckhard, R., and Pritchard, W. *Changing the Essence: The Art of Creating and Leading Environmental Change in Organizations.* San Francisco: Jossey-Bass, 1992.

Bennis, W., and Nanus, B. *Leaders: The Strategies for Taking Charge.* New York: HarperCollins, 1985.

Bolman, L. G., and Deal, T. E. *Leading with Soul: An Uncommon Journey of Spirit.* San Francisco: Jossey-Bass, 1995.

Block, P. *Stewardship.* San Francisco: Berrett-Koehler, 1993.

Bridges, W. *Managing Transitions: Making the Most of Change.* Reading, Mass.: Addison-Wesley, 1991.

Chittister, J. *Wisdom Distilled from the Daily.* New York: HarperCollins, 1990.

Collins, J., and Porras, J. *Built to Last.* New York: HarperCollins, 1994.

Creech, B. *The Five Pillars of TQM.* New York: Truman Talley, 1994.

Crosby, P. B. *Quality Is Free.* New York: McGraw-Hill, 1979.

Deming, W. E. *Out of the Crisis.* Cambridge, Mass.: MIT Center for Advanced Engineering Study, 1986.

Deming, W. E. *The New Economics.* Cambridge, Mass.: MIT Center for Advanced Engineering Study, 1994.

Fulghum, R. "Pay Attention." In R. Carlson and B. Shield (eds.), *Handbook for the Soul.* Boston: Little, Brown, 1995.

Gardner, J. W. *On Leadership.* New York: Macmillan, 1990.

Garvin, D. "Building a Learning Organization." *Harvard Business Review,* July–August 1993, pp. 78–91.

Gleick, J. *Chaos.* New York: Viking, 1987.

Goldstein, J. *The Unshackled Organization.* Portland, Oreg.: Productivity Press, 1995.

Greenleaf, R. *Servant Leadership.* Mahwah, N.J.: Paulist, 1977.

Juran, J. M. *Juran on Planning for Quality.* New York: Free Press, 1988.

Kellert, S. *In the Wake of Chaos.* Chicago: University of Chicago, 1993.

Kelly, K. *Out of Control.* Reading, Mass.: Addison-Wesley, 1994.

Kline, P., and Saunders, B. *Ten Steps to a Learning Organization.* Arlington, Va.: Great Ocean, 1993.

Lorenz, E. *The Essence of Chaos.* Seattle: University of Washington Press, 1993.

Marquardt, M., and Reynolds, A. *The Global Learning Organization.* Burr Ridge, Ill.: Irwin, 1994.

McGill, M., and Slocum, J. *The Smarter Organization.* New York: Wiley, 1994.

Mitroff, I., and Linstone, H. *The Unbounded Mind.* New York: Oxford University, 1993.

Morgan, G. *Images of Organizations.* Thousand Oaks, Calif.: Sage, 1986.

Nanus, B. *The Leader's Edge.* Chicago: Contemporary Books, 1989.

O'Toole, J. *Leading Change: Overcoming the Ideology of Comfort and the Tyranny of Custom.* San Francisco: Jossey-Bass, 1995.

Peters, T. *The Pursuit of Wow!* New York: Vintage Books, 1994.

Richards, D. *Artful Work.* San Francisco: Berrett-Koehler, 1995.

Schein, E. *Organizational Culture and Leadership.* San Francisco: Jossey-Bass, 1992.

Senge, P. "The Leader's New Work: Building Learning Organizations." *Sloan Management Review,* 1990, 32 (1), 7–23.

Senge, P. *The Fifth Discipline.* New York: Doubleday, 1992.

Senge, P., Roberts, C., Ross, R., Smith, B., and Kleiner, A. *The Fifth Discipline Fieldbook: Strategies and Tools for Building a Learning Organization.* New York: Doubleday, 1994.

Spears, L. (ed.). *Reflections on Leadership.* New York: Wiley, 1995.

Stacey, R. D. *Managing the Unknowable: Strategic Boundaries Between Order and Chaos in Organizations.* San Francisco: Jossey-Bass, 1992.

Swieringa, J., and Wierdsma, A. *Becoming a Learning Organization.* Reading, Mass.: Addison-Wesley, 1992.

Useem, M., and Kochan, T. "Creating the Learning Organization." In T. Kochan and M. Useem (eds.), *Transforming Organizations.* New York: Oxford University, 1992.

Walton, M. *The Deming Management Method.* New York: Putnam, 1986.

Watkins, K. E., and Marsick, V. J. *Sculpting the Learning Organization: Lessons in the Art and Science of Systematic Change.* San Francisco: Jossey-Bass, 1993.

Wheatley, M. *Leadership and the New Science.* San Francisco: Berrett-Koehler, 1992.

CURT KOCHNER is director of student life and housing at Montana State University–Billings.

TIMOTHY R. MCMAHON is assistant professor in the Department of Counselor Education and College Student Personnel at Western Illinois University.

*Most educators would acknowledge that there is significant room
for quality improvement in higher education. Quality should be
approached through continuous improvement aimed at seeking better
ways of meeting or exceeding the demands placed on the educational
system by customers.*

Some Final Thoughts on Achieving Quality

William A. Bryan

Continuous quality improvement (CQI) expectations from different constituencies (internal and external) will constantly confront campuses in the
future. The higher education debate regarding the value of TQM persists while
consumer expectations and institutional pursuit of CQI continue.

This volume has attempted to provide a balanced coverage of TQM and
to inform student affairs professionals of issues surrounding its use. Chapter
authors have presented differing perspectives on TQM and have provided
examples of its application to student affairs work functions. The focus of this
volume has been to examine the advantages and disadvantages of TQM and
not to present a theme of acceptance or rejection of its principles. An alterna-
tive to TQM, "the learning organization" (Senge, 1992), is highlighted exten-
sively in Chapter Seven.

This chapter presents ideas regarding what quality is not and an examination of why student affairs professionals must strive for quality. It offers some
thoughts on why TQM may fail in efforts to establish it on campus. A series of
questions that student affairs professionals may wish to explore as they seek to
implement a quality approach is outlined. The importance of a concerted commitment to quality as the key ingredient to the development of a strong campus community is presented.

Striving for Quality

As discussed in Chapter One of this volume, there is a growing concern for
quality in the campus setting. The higher education environment is changing,
competition for funding and students is increasing, and we are under pressure

NEW DIRECTIONS FOR STUDENT SERVICES, no. 76, Winter 1996 © Jossey-Bass Publishers to find ways of doing more with less (Lewis and Smith, 1994). In the U.S. education is being scrutinized as never before. In Chapter Six, Scott states that the "public outcry is for more accountability and quality" on the campus. Parents are paying higher tuition bills, legislators "are facing more public demand for services and programs," and students are demanding more accountability and quality from higher education institutions.

Howard, in Chapter Two, notes that student affairs professionals are dedicated to meeting the needs of students (customers) rather than assuming that they know what is best for students—this has been the typical higher education response. Seeking opinions from students through interviews and surveys is a common practice for student affairs professionals; typically, they are very concerned with assessment and evaluation of their plans and activities.

Kochner and McMahon in Chapter Seven suggest that educators must move from "do more with less" to "do different with less." They do not believe that it is reasonable to demand more from less staff with less budget. This practice will destroy an organization. They also suggest that educators must "do different with more." The *more* they refer to is technology, knowledgeable staff, diversity, and collecting "information about what conditions foster student learning." Holmes, in Chapter Three, supports a strong commitment to the development of student affairs staff in order to promote effective student learning and services.

Mullendore and Wang (Chapter Four) make a strong case for the unification of "individuals, processes, functional areas, and units into a complex and integrated process" that promotes a comprehensive planning model "that can help connect reporting, planning, budgeting, and assessment." The challenge they outline is how to integrate programs and services with the institutional mission and goals.

To provide quality services and educational opportunities for students, student affairs departments must develop partnerships with other higher-education units. Through collaboration and the pursuit of partnerships with those best able to help in the development of excellence, student affairs educators can best serve their customers. The value and effectiveness of student affairs programs and services can only be enhanced through partnering with other educators. Bogue and Saunders (1992) state that "no one who has taken the journey toward improved quality concludes that journey without acknowledging the need for partnership" (p. 216).

A division of student affairs striving for CQI promotes division renewal that will upgrade practices, leading to improved services and programs for students. Such a division is constantly seeking new and better ways of working. The renewal process calls for a changing organization road map to produce quality services and educational opportunities for students.

What the Pursuit of Quality Is Not

Quality does not just happen: quality, as a result, is not unintentional. In Chapter One, I suggest that some educators see TQM approaches as too structured and mechanical. For quality to occur, however, there cannot be an unstructured approach to the pursuit of quality. A quality structure is not hierarchical, does not base decisions on assumptions, does not exclude staff in the decision making process, and does not exclude customer opinion in formulating decisions. In the pursuit of quality, organizations must be proactive in the search for new and better ways of working.

Hutton (1994, pp. 306–309) outlines what quality is not. Quality is not a project or a program. There is no end to the pursuit of quality; it is a continuous journey for the search of new and better ways of providing services. It is not an additional part of the job educators do, but a vital part in the design of work. Quality is not an afterthought. The pursuit of quality by an organization is not a public relations ploy; it is about creating services and educational opportunities that meet or exceed customer needs or desires. A quick fix to a problem should not be expected. The search for quality is a long-term organizational commitment that requires perseverance and dedicated work focused on improvement. Furthermore, it is not a cure-all; success is not guaranteed. The pursuit of quality in a student affairs division can benefit activities in the organization, but it is not wizardry.

Why TQM Fails

Kochner and McMahon (Chapter Seven) suggest that TQM literature does not properly address the role of the leader in an organization. The leader's responsibility of adapting to external changes and setting new and creative directions is generally neglected. Further, they say that the concepts of vision and mission are rarely mentioned. Vision is usually "not seen as a guiding force of leadership, but as a management tool." A leader's vision, style, and ability to adapt to new demands in a fast-paced changing world are all important.

Although most educators realize that change is something they will continually face in their job setting, resistance to change is a major obstacle to carrying out TQM (Howard, Chapter Two). Many people do not understand the need for change and often resist it. As Nancy Lee Howard states in Chapter Two of this volume, resistance is generally present "when the need for specific change is not apparent to those affected by the changes." Like Brown, Hitchcock, and Willard (1994), Howard notes that TQM "requires the commitment of time and resources" and a long-term focus. Many practitioners are frustrated with the time commitment required to learn and apply TQM concepts and do not have patience for long-term strategies. They feel that they are being taken away from their real commitments. In student affairs divisions, money is generally scarce and staffs are overextended, but there must be an investment in staff training and education.

Also, Howard suggests that TQM will not work in dysfunctional work units. Trust and openness to change are key ingredients for TQM to thrive, as is an open, unrestricted communication system within the institution (Seymour, 1995). Institutional barriers to communication must be recognized and removed if a customer's wants and needs are to be understood and addressed appropriately.

In Chapter Three, Holmes states that educational institutions must pursue improved program outcomes, not merely the enhancement and stabilization of the processes that lead to the outcomes. He suggests that process improvement has become the primary focus in many organizations and not the impact of processes on desired organizational outcomes. He believes that outcome goals are not always met even though process improvement is accomplished. Further, he states that many TQM efforts create bureaucratic structures that prevent employee empowerment and the encouragement of creativity and teamwork.

For higher education, there are barriers to TQM that can lead to its failure. Holmes states that terminology such as statistical process control (SPC), "cause-and-effect diagrams, *kaizen,* benchmarking, common-cause variation, and plan-do-check-act cycles" is commonly used in TQM. "With the exception of business and engineering faculty, however," states Holmes, "such terms are foreign to most [educators]." In general, the organizational structure of higher education institutions is different from business; education institutions are generally not top-down, hierarchical organizations, but are more democratic in nature. He sees educational institutions as having "multiple spheres of influence existing at a variety of levels" within the institution. Holmes also suggests that many faculty see TQM as the latest management fad and believe that it will be short-lived.

Many authors in this volume underscore the importance of top leadership's commitment to and understanding of TQM principles. Key leaders must "walk the talk." Why is top leadership attracted to TQM? Brown, Hitchcock, and Willard (1994) state that leaders "are sometimes attracted to TQM for the wrong reasons. Their customers may demand it or executives may mistake TQM as purely a cost-cutting strategy" (p. 2). Waiting until there is an institutional financial crisis will only limit resources needed for TQM's proper implementation. Higher education leaders must know how to support the use of TQM or any quality program. They must understand that what they express through attitudes, actions, and words will greatly affect a campus community's commitment to the use of TQM. "It is clear that managers cannot fake the new paradigm by knowing the 'right words' or practicing the 'right style'" (Brown, Hitchcock, and Willard, 1994, p. 163).

Implementing a Quality System

Many limitations of TQM have been addressed in this volume. Lewis and Smith (1994, p. 234) note that there is a "rich and diverse milieu" of quality models for implementing quality on campus. There is no single quality model designed to meet the needs, expectations, and demands of every higher education environment; therefore, educators must be aware of the strengths and weaknesses of any quality approach. They must be prepared to alter or design a quality model to fit the unique aspects of their campus culture. Awareness of the possible limitations of TQM or any other quality model will enable higher education leaders to make adjustments that can only strengthen their pursuit of campus quality.

Whatever quality approach is used, the goal is total integration into the campus culture, so that it is a way of life in the daily operation of the campus. From the beginning of an institution's quest for quality, the beliefs and behaviors of campus leadership can herald the development of an outstanding campus quality system or doom it to failure. Outlined below are questions that student affairs professionals should answer when considering implementing a quality approach:

Are leaders supportive and committed to tireless work for quality?
Does leadership accept the responsibility of adapting to external changes and setting new and innovative directions for the organization?
Is leadership shared?
What values are seen as basic?
Has a mission statement been developed and is it understood by community members?
Has a vision statement been developed and is there a shared understanding of its meaning?
Have customers been identified?
Are all employees involved in the process?
Is there an emphasis on the widespread, extensive involvement of staff?
Do staff members have a long-term commitment to quality?
Are staff members helped to understand the need for change?
Do staff feel empowered to make their own decisions, work standards, and goals; organize their work; and deal directly with customers?
Is there support for the professional development of student affairs staff?
Is trust present?
Is the organizational structure conducive to learning on a daily basis through debate and discussion?
Is there awareness that the organization is an entity in which everything influences everything else?
Is the quality model or approach too structured or mechanical?
Is there a pervasive understanding of why quality is important?
Does everyone understand and accept the terminology being used?
Is there open examination of underlying assumptions and beliefs to improve results?
Is there an understanding of the time and energy necessary for success?
Is there acceptance of the basic tenet that any process can and should be improved?
Is the focus of a problem on the process?
Is information free-flowing and accurate, with emphasis on needed data and facts?

Are quality initiatives geared toward the facilitation of student service, learn-
ing, and development?
Is the quality structure being created cumbersome and bureaucratic?
Are teams the cornerstone of the quality approach?
Is there an understanding that there must be attention to outcomes and the
improvement of processes?
Is there an awareness that cultural changes in the institution will be necessary?

By leadership seeking responses to many of these questions, insight can
be gained into the climate and readiness of a campus to pursue the development of a campus quality system. TQM is not the answer for a dysfunctional
department; it can only improve a communicative and functional system.
Many TQM gurus identified in this volume view the quest for quality differently and offer diverse options for consideration. There are multiple
approaches to implementing TQM. Lewis and Smith (1994) say that "in sum,
the strategy advocated . . . is an eclectic hybrid of all . . . approaches: taking
the best and configuring it into a framework . . . most applicable to the higher
educational environment" (p. 236). The question a campus quality leader must
answer is: What approach is most applicable to my campus and its unique culture?

Conclusion

This sourcebook has explored TQM themes, tools, and beliefs; negatives and
positives; and strengths and weaknesses in an educational environment. It has
outlined a comprehensive planning model in a student affairs division that
integrates TQM principles, described a systematic approach used in one student affairs division to introduce TQM into its culture, and given examples of
the importance of assessment in TQM. The reader has also been introduced to
aspects of organizational development that TQM does not effectively address.
Student affairs professionals are key players in the building of a strong
campus community. Is there a link between building community and quality?
Bogue and Saunders (1992) state that "without community one will find nei-
ther caring nor courtesy, and without caring, there will be no quality, for there
will be no standards" (p. 23). As Gardner (1990) suggests, the strength of a
campus community determines the level of accomplishment of its purposes.
Bogue and Saunders (1992) suggest that the 1990 publication of the Carnegie
Foundation for the Advancement of Teaching, *Campus Life: In Search of Community,* speaks to the issue of quality in higher education. Basic principles and
beliefs related to quality are addressed in each chapter:

First, a college or university is an educationally purposeful community—a place
where faculty and students share academic goals and work together to
strengthen teaching and learning on the campus. Second, a college or university
is an open community—a place where freedom of expression is uncompromis-

ingly protected and where civility is powerfully affirmed. Third, a college or university is a just community, a place where the sacredness of the person is honored and where diversity is aggressively pursued. Fourth, a college or university is a disciplined community, a place where individuals accept their obligations to the group and where well-defined governance procedures guide behavior for the common good. Fifth, a college or university is a caring community—a place where the well-being of each member is sensitively supported and where service to others is encouraged. Sixth, a college or university is a celebrative community in which the heritage of the institution is remembered and where rituals affirming both tradition and change are widely shared [pp. 7–8].

If educators accept these principles and beliefs regarding community, then they recognize the importance of quality in the daily life of the campus. What educator would argue against quality? The concerns about quality center around the answers given to the characteristics named above. In the pursuit of quality, educators must be partners in developing quality strategies and dealing with difficult questions in an open arena. The right focus is the pursuit of quality for the sake of students, with the recognition that leaders must be sensitive to the differences within each campus culture. As the TQM literature suggests, there are many different avenues to quality.

References

Bogue, E. G., and Saunders, R. L. *The Evidence for Quality: Strengthening the Tests of Academic and Administrative Effectiveness.* San Francisco: Jossey-Bass, 1992.

Brown, M. G., Hitchcock, D. E., and Willard, M. L. *Why TQM Fails and What to Do About It.* Burr Ridge, Ill.: Irwin, 1994.

Carnegie Foundation for the Advancement of Teaching. *Campus Life: In Search of Community.* Princeton, N.J.: Princeton University Press, 1990.

Gardner, J. W. *On Leadership.* New York: Macmillan, 1990.

Hutton, D. W. *The Change Agents' Handbook.* Milwaukee, Wis.: ASQC Quality Press, 1994.

Lewis, R. G., and Smith, D. H. *Total Quality in Higher Education.* Delray Beach, Fla.: St. Lucie Press, 1994.

Senge, P. *The Fifth Discipline.* New York: Doubleday, 1992.

Seymour, D. *Once Upon a Campus: Lessons for Improving Quality and Productivity in Higher Education.* Phoenix, Ariz.: American Council on Education and Oryx Press, 1995.

WILLIAM A. BRYAN is professor of specialty studies at the University of North Carolina at Wilmington. He served as chief student affairs officer for eighteen years and is a former president of the American College Personnel Association.

INDEX

Ordering Information

New Directions for Student Services is a series of paperback books that offers guidelines and programs for aiding students in their total development—emotional, social, and physical, as well as intellectual. Books in the series are published quarterly in Spring, Summer, Fall, and Winter and are available for purchase by subscription as well as individually.

Subscriptions cost $52.00 for individuals (a savings of 35 percent over single-copy prices) and $79.00 for institutions, agencies, and libraries. Standing orders are accepted. New York residents, add local sales tax for subscriptions. (For subscriptions outside the United States, add $7.00 for shipping via surface mail or $25.00 for air mail. Orders *must be prepaid* in U.S. dollars by check drawn on a U.S. bank or charged to VISA, MasterCard, or American Express.)

Single copies cost $20.00 plus shipping (see below) when payment accompanies order. California, New Jersey, New York, and Washington, D.C., residents, please include appropriate sales tax. Canadian residents, add GST and any local taxes. Billed orders will be charged shipping and handling. No billed shipments to post office boxes. (Orders from outside the United States *must be prepaid* by check drawn on a U.S. bank or charged to VISA, MasterCard, or American Express.)

Shipping (single copies only): one issue, add $5.00; two issues, add $6.00; three issues, add $7.00; four to five issues, add $8.00; six to seven issues, add $9.00; eight or more issues, add $12.00.

All prices are subject to change.

Discounts for quantity orders are available. Please write to the address below for information.

All orders must include either the name of an individual or an official purchase order number. Please submit your order as follows:
  Subscriptions: specify series and year subscription is to begin
  Single copies: include individual title code (such as SS55)

Mail all orders to:
  Jossey-Bass Publishers
  350 Sansome Street
  San Francisco, California 94104-1342

For subscription sales outside of the United States, contact any international subscription agency or Jossey-Bass directly.

OTHER TITLES AVAILABLE IN THE
NEW DIRECTIONS FOR STUDENT SERVICES SERIES
Margaret J. Barr, Editor-in-Chief
M. Lee Upcraft, Associate Editor